Wild Kent
its nature and landscape

Edited by: James Teacher and Pete Raine
Principal photographers: John and Irene Palmer

Published by the Kent Wildlife Trust to celebrate its 40th anniversary

Published in Great Britain by the Kent Wildlife Trust 1998
ISBN: 0 950 44092 2

Printed by Geerings of Ashford Ltd.

Wild Kent

its nature and landscape

KENT - this map shows the location of the 40 reserves in this book

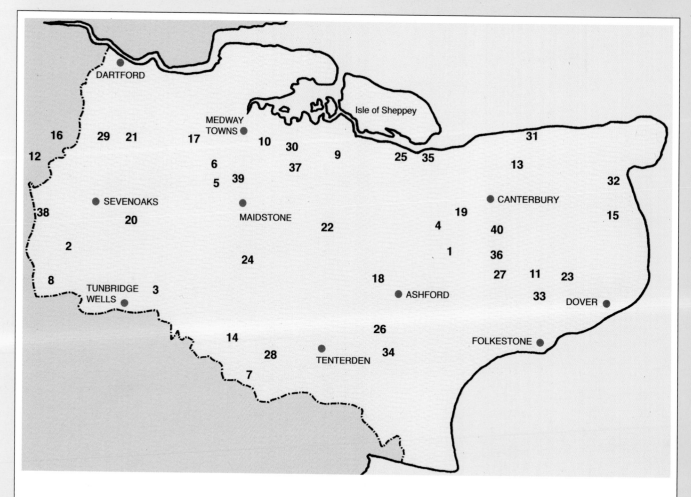

Kent Wildlife Trust was founded as a charity in 1958 and works to protect Kent's wildlife and wild places. If you would like further information about nature reserves, volunteering, membership or any aspect of the Trust's work, please contact us at **Tyland Barn, Sandling, Maidstone ME14 8AX. Phone 01622.662012.**

CONTENTS

Moonrise over Oare Marshes

FOREWORD

THIS BOOK commemorates forty years of the Kent Wildlife Trust and is dedicated to the wisdom and foresight of those who saw the speed of change of farming practice and urbanisation as a severe threat to our lovely county and decided to do something about it. It may be invidious to mention names but Hector Wilks, Chairman of the Trust for twenty years and his friends Andrew Ruck, Francis Rose and Deryk Fraser and our former President, almost since the Trust's inception, Lord Brabourne, would rank high in our roll of honour.

Then we should remember the enigmatic personality of Iris Darnton of Sissinghurst Court whose huge benefaction enabled the Trust to fulfil many of its cherished projects which, but for her, would have remained the stuff of dreams.

The Trust has been fortunate in its Directors. First Fred Booth whose solid reassuring presence during difficult times enabled us to build the firm base from which the mercurial character of Pete Raine could not only move us into Tyland Barn but propel us firmly into the centre of county environmental politics. Neither of them could have been effective without a dedicated staff whose unfailing good humour and genial banter belie the great efficiency and the seriousness with which they undertake their duties.

We should not forget the members whose extreme generosity we rely on time and time again, particularly for the purchase and management of reserves; nor could we do without the help of the trustees of the many charities who support our work, as do government bodies such as English Nature and the National Heritage Lottery Fund. Volunteers give up thousands of hours of their free time to help the work of the Trust. We can attribute the high standard of the conservation work on our reserves to their dedication.

Thank you all.

It has been my unenviable task to edit this book. The contributions are extraordinary in their variety. I have endeavoured to maintain their character and style but I have had to make some changes in order to make room for and sense of the illustrations. For instance Bill Oddie's love of birds is such that he writes about Sandwich - one of the great botanical sites - without mentioning a single plant! I hope he will forgive me for planting a few in the sand dunes, damp hollows and shingle beaches of Sandwich Bay.

The photographers are all members of the Trust and have produced work of great beauty that truly reflects the natural wonders of our county.

I hope this book will encourage people to visit our reserves. They are places of enormous interest, often isolated, generally peaceful - places to refresh the soul in this bustling world. Above all this book is a celebration of the wildlife of Kent

James Teacher
Chairman of KWT 1985 - 1998

Tyland Barn

The teaching shelter

VISIONS are, at best, only partially fulfilled. I first saw Tyland Barn on a wet December afternoon in 1989, and in the months that followed, a variety of dreams were sketched out on our mental drawing boards.

We knew we needed a new and permanent headquarters to form a secure base for the Trust for years to come. We wanted a high profile public visitor centre to act as a showcase for the wildlife of the county. We envisaged a natural park with a variety of habitats to replace the overgrown field of grass that flanked the barn. We thought that there might be a market for a wildlife education centre for use by schools. Finally, we hoped, as we contemplated the rotten timbers, leaking corrugated iron roof and mud floor, that we would be able to convert this dilapidated 300 year old barn into a workable modern building.

Nine years on, we can look back with some pride. Council made a commendably robust decision to lease the building and convert it into offices in April 1990, and by the end of that year a feasibility study had been drawn up and fundraising was well under way. Work started in July 1991, and we moved in in August 1992. Throughout this period, I was grateful for the support of Council and staff, but especially for the constant commitment of James Teacher and Hector Wilks.

Tyland Barn is a striking conversion that still retains character and a sense of place. As an office, it works well; although we knew we would eventually need to expand into the outbuildings. The fact that we did so only four years after moving in to the main Barn is a sign of the rate of expansion of the Trust's activities as well as the welcome funding opportunity afforded by the Heritage Lottery Fund. The natural park has exceeded our expectations, with a well established pond and maturing trees and shrubs - breeding frogs, newts and a pair of whitethroats are evidence of success.

As a public visitor centre, the Barn has not quite lived up to the early vision, with only 15,000 visitors a year who are, however, unstinting in their praise of the welcome they receive. The educational side has gone better than even an optimist like me could have dared to hope. A staggering 5000 schoolchildren on study days are expected in 19.98.

Much hard work went into making Tyland Barn what it is today. I can think of no better return on that investment than the sight of young faces lighting up at their first sight of a dragonfly, a hawkmoth, or a hive full of bees. Long may it continue.

Pete Raine
Director of KWT, 1989 -1998

Bonsai Bank

VIEW Bonsai Bank as one of the best reserves for the simple reason that it introduced me to the world of lepidoptera and in particular the thirty species of butterfly which roam the site every spring and summer. Until I started recording butterflies on the transect as the honorary warden of the reserve I would not have been able to differentiate between a red admiral and a rear admiral. Some might say that I still can't. It did not add to my natural history reputation when during the first year of recording I noted that I had seen some thirty or so pearl bordered fritillaries over a period of a few weeks when others had seen a

Lady orchid

mere one or two during their adult flight period. Alarm bells rang with the cognoscenti when they surmised their novice recorder was either notching up the results without actually going anywhere near the site or alternatively did not recognise a pearl bordered when he saw one. Fortunately my integrity was restored if not my natural history prowess when it was accepted that I had mistaken the speckled yellow moth for a pearl bordered. Sadly none has been recorded on the transect although a number of lepidopterists have reported seeing them since. I have been recording for six years now and hopefully improved my butterfly recognition. When I saw a Camberwell beauty on the transect last year it was accepted without demur.

The butterfly numbers seen during the year are not high in comparison to other sites where transects are done. Bonsai has, though, a wide variety of species which are generally seen on the site year on year from five different species of skipper to a host of marbled whites which herald high summer. Keen lepidopterists visit the site from all over the south of England in May and June to find the Duke of Burgundy fritillary a somewhat dullish chequered patterned, charming little butterfly with much of the perky behaviour of the hairstreak. It was known in the eighteenth century as Mr. Vernon's small fritillary from its resemblance to the fritillaries in pattern although it is in fact the only representative in Europe of a different family, - the *Riodinidae*. Others of the family are more colourful and usually found in South America. Increasingly a rare species in this country it lives in small, closely knit colonies in woodland clearings where either the cowslip or primrose grow, the latter being abundant at Bonsai Bank. The colony on this 20 acre site consists of a couple of hundred

Duke of Burgundy fritillary

Dingy skipper

individuals. Last year (1997) forty two adults were recorded on the transect during their flight period over a period of five weeks in May and early June, the maximum for any year since records have been kept.

The site is managed on behalf of Forestry Enterprise, under a twenty year lease with the primary aim of managing it for the Duke of Burgundies and orchids of which five species are regularly seen - the rare lady orchid, early purple, common spotted, the butterfly and common twayblade.

The west facing chalk site gained its name from the conifers in the early sixties with which it was planted. Rabbits stunted the growth of many of

Blue fleabane

loud far-carrying cry of the green woodpecker or the rich song of the nightingale nearer to hand. It is visited by comparatively few persons except at times when the Duke of Burgundy is in flight or orchids are in bloom. One reason may be that it is a brisk twenty minute walk from the road. Unlike the friend of George Bernard Shaw who never missed an occasion to let slip an opportunity, do visit Bonsai Bank. The effort is worth it.

Richard Margrie
Honorary Warden

them by eating the tops. Hence the name by which the reserve is now known. It was fenced around its perimeter three years ago. The intention of the fence was that cows, sheep or goats could graze the site. It was arranged for a grazier to put a number of goats on the site. Two only were ever present and spent more of their time jumping over the electric fence which was erected to create various sections. The goats never managed to escape from the reserve itself but the experiment has not been repeated.

Bonsai Bank must be one of the quietest KWT reserves. On a summer afternoon or evening the only sound that can often be heard is the hoot of the tawny owl on the other side of the valley, the

Greater butterfly orchid

Bough Beech

Dawn at the edge of Bough Beech reservoir

THIS water storage reservoir was constructed in the 1960s. The first flash flood of water was in January 1969 attracting 70 mallard.

Frank Brightman, the then chairman of the Trust's Conservation Committee, invited me to attend the inaugural meeting with the owners, East Surrey Water Company. There I met their Chief Engineer, Gordon Swales, who was to say the least, a formidable gentleman. His first words to me were "Well Coles, what are your qualifications to study the birds" - oh dear? - "Well, Sir, to be rude to trespassers and polite to the management" . He liked that.

I found myself appointed honorary warden and secretary to the management committee. After which Frank Brightman invited me to attend meetings of the Trust's conservation committee, and I eventually joined Council.

Andrew Ruck took a regular interest in this new reserve. The Trust was growing up at this time, having dropped the name Kent Naturalist's Trust, because of the confusion with sunbathers! Tony Wilson was engaged as Conservation Officer. Those three people, together with Gordon Williams the reservoir superintendent got me off to a good start with various projects, such as dams to hold water back as the level dropped after the

Winter sunset

Kingfisher

Great crested grebe

winter rains. I found I was quickly joined by a bank of enthusiastic volunteers. Some of them are still with me, crippled of course! Together we created the wader pits and reed beds and a variety of habitats. Two dipping ponds with safe platforms to work from have proved very interesting, being extensively used by school parties.

Fortunately most of the area can be viewed from a raised causeway road which bisects the reserve. Visitors are able to watch the courtship and nesting of great crested grebe and little ringed plover. LRPs are our number one bird as they usually nest quite close to the road. An innovation at Bough Beech has been the use of 3" mesh cages to protect the eggs from carrion crows and other predators. The cages are placed over after the clutch is completed. During incubation the adult LRPs run unconcerned through the mesh at change over time.

One of my best days was in the spring of 1976. Some winter rains left vast areas of bare clay and there were eleven nests of little ringed plover, two of ringed plover, several lapwing, three nest boxes of tawny owl and four of kestrel plus various warblers. They were joined by a pair of Kentish plovers which stayed all

Little ringed plover chick

day - would they nest? The problems of protecting them occupied my mind until the next morning - when they had gone. That day had been memorable with a passage of a dozen curlew and several each of whimbrel, greenshank, common sandpiper, green sandpiper, redshank, ruff, common tern, whinchat and redstart.

The Company gave the Trust use of an old oast house. This has been developed into a visitor centre, introducing local history and nature conservation to the visiting public and frequent organised school parties. Currently under the leadership of Joan Medill the centre is staffed by volunteers with several thousand visitors each year.

Development of the reserve continues. Recently a floating otter holt has been installed and a roadside nature reserve is being monitored by Hilary Streeter.

Up to 65 bird species nest each year and the total of birds recorded is 240 to date. On a spring morning it's possible to see, with luck, seventy species from the causeway. Rare birds turn up - Radde's warbler 1984 was the first inland record for Kent. Another first for Kent was a little crake 1997.

Roy Coles
Photographer and Honorary Warden

Brenchley Wood

Dunnock feeding fledgling cuckoo

OUR first visit to Brenchley Wood was in the autumn of 1974, shown around by the warden, Brian Mitchell. This was just five years after the Kent Wildlife Trust had purchased the 7˙ acres of relict High Weald woodland that made up the reserve. The most important feature of the wood was that it was wet and included a sphagnum flush at its northern end. More than twenty five bryophytes had been listed along with one hundred or so vascular plants and a good bird list was soon added.

It took us at least a couple of hours to complete the walk, along a network of paths zig-zagging up and down wet slopes and through this amazingly varied and fascinating patch of woodland. It was surely more than just seven acres in extent and this was the comment that Sue and I continued to hear so many times from the scores of groups that we took around, once we had become wardens ourselves.

As in most woodlands, spring is the best time and so many people visiting then will have been enchanted by its diversity - orange tip and brimstone butterflies along the ride, four warbler species in song, woodpeckers drumming and sunny patches of wood anemones and opposite-leaved golden saxifrage. Most of all, the wood is quiet and peaceful.

The reserve now consists of 23 acres with the addition of the adjoining Foxhole Wood which was

Mating orange tip butterflies

Great spotted woodpecker

purchased in 1994 following an amazingly successful local appeal to raise the necessary cash. It is now an even more varied reserve with hazel coppice and some fine oak standards on the slopes, a small area of old beech, sweet chestnut coppice, alder on the lower wet areas adjacent to Tudeley Brook and a plantation of Scots pine which is currently being cleared to encourage heathland vegetation to flourish. A fine ride has been cleared through the entire length of the wood making a great walk from Foxhole Lane and linking up with Tunbridge Wells Council's Cinderhill community woodland. This long break in the canopy has encouraged many more butterflies and birds of the woodland edge.

Our time associated with Brenchley and Foxhole woods has been an interesting one. We watched in disbelief as our neighbours planted a lovely heathland slope along our old boundary with Scots pine which now, nineteen years later is part of the reserve and which we are clearing to attempt to recreate this rare habitat in Kent. It is

amazing how the heather has survived and is growing through well!

The great storm of October 1987 hit Brenchley Wood as hard as it did many other woodlands in the south east, and much of our management time in the following few years was spent in re-opening paths and clearing fallen timber. Although it was a great shock at the time and we were very upset, time has healed the scars. We reckon that the reserve has benefited in the long term, with the canopy opened up and glades enlarged. We have certainly recorded more butterflies and one of the plants that responded immediately was the marsh valerian which flowered profusely as soon as the light came in. We also met Pete Raine for the first time. He had been

Wood horsetail

Blackbird

appointed to advise on and co-ordinate the Trust's efforts after the storm.

Weather patterns have certainly changed in the years that we have known Brenchley Wood and the generally hot dry summers have adversely affected the wetland flora of the reserve. Changes in land use have been great along our western boundary over the years. Old orchards were grubbed out, boggy fields were drained and some hedgerows removed. Our bird populations have definitely declined in this time along with the dramatic changes in agriculture throughout the country. We rarely see spotted flycatchers here now, yellowhammers seem to have gone and we only have a few song thrushes and even fewer bullfinches.

Don't let this stop you from paying a visit, however; we still have three species of woodpecker, nuthatch and treecreeper, five species of warbler, woodcock, sparrowhawk, kestrel, tawny owl and many more. We may even have nightjar and stonechat to offer in the future as our heath is extended along with neighbouring Cinderhill Wood.

Our springtime flowers and butterflies look great on sunny days as the new bright green leaf canopy begins to unfurl. On an early morning walk you might see a fox along the open ride or even encounter a badger from a nearby sett noisily enjoying a drink in the brook in the middle of the afternoon. If you don't manage to see one of the reserve's mammals you can certainly enjoy a blackcap's song in the peace and tranquillity of this unusual spot, which we ourselves continue to love and enjoy.

John & Sue Buckingham
Photographers and Honorary Wardens

Broadham Down

A distant view of Broadham Down

I AM told that the first Council party to visit Broadham got hopelessly lost before they found it. Not so surprising as it is one of the those discreet reserves that are tucked up tortuous lanes. What is more, they were looking for a down and found a dogwood forest. As our Green Team peeled away that coat of scrub all sorts of exciting things were revealed - an old farm which "disappeared" during the last century with its attendant well; a denehole that is used by Daubenton, Natterer's and brown long-eared bats; and a wonderful flora with superb colonies of man orchid and typical downland views.

Blackveined moth - a rare species restricted in Kent to the area round Broadham Down

Green lane at the base of Broadham Down

Nettle leaved bellflower

I live about three hundred yards from Broadham Down. I would like to emphasise how enjoyable it is to work as a member of a Green Team, and the satisfaction gained from the work other volunteers and myself have done on the down is enormous.

The first thing you learn on your first day on a task is that you are out of shape. A Green Team task will teach you about muscles only otherwise discoverable in an anatomy class. There is a kind of perverse but real pleasure in reckoning up the aches and pains and noticing how they decrease the more tasks you show up for. And then there is the pleasure of knowing that there are benefits for nature, wildlife and your fellow human beings.

Imagine you are walking up a lane to the top of Broadham Down. The Green Team, ten or twelve of you, are tackling the scrub for the first time. You get to the top of the down and WHAM! You're expecting some sort of vista. What you get

Mating gatekeeper butterflies

Greenbottle fly

much. You show up for the second day's work and at the end you say to yourselves, 'May be - may be we'll make it'. At the end of the third day you say to yourself, 'We're going to do this. It's going to be touch and go, but we're going to get this finished by the end of April'. And the team does finish it, as near as dammit. Now I go up there and see the orchids and the downland prospering and there is the pride and pleasure of saying to yourself, 'I had a hand in this'.

Roger Hardy
Volunteer member of the KWT Green Team

•

is a ten foot wall of dogwood, hazel and thorn. You know that you're supposed to clear about 16 acres by the end of April. You look at the other people's faces. Everyone is attempting to exhibit impassivity in the face of apparent impossibility. You adjust your own mask. Work starts. You renew acquaintances - you make new friends. The females on the team are doing as much work, and having as good a time as the males. You survey the day's work. Groan. Not

Burham Down

Mignonette colonising slopes newly cleared of scrub

"'M taking my lunch up to Burham," I said as I left the office. The still, sunny, July day and the need to write this article provided me with the perfect excuse.

Parking in the KCC Bluebell Hill Picnic Site, high on the North Downs, I noted that several other cars were parked up against the bank, their occupants mostly still inside admiring the view.

Armed with flower book, insect book, binoculars and lunch I set off to the west. The reserve is divided into three sections including two disused chalk pits and has several access points. A stile, fence and Nature Reserve sign marked my point of entry and I sat, alone with my thoughts.

The view was impressive: the villages of Burham and Eccles, fields of golden corn, dark green wooded areas, the River Medway meandering across with the tide obviously in, the motorway, suburban houses and vast swathes of rather conspicuous white-roofed factories and

Fairy flax

warehouses. A shame, I thought, that they couldn't have made them green or brown. Marching into the distance were electricity pylons, reminding me of the one at the foot of the hill which is shortly to be moved to accommodate the Channel Tunnel Rail Link - which itself will run beneath this hillside.

Immediately below, the old chalk pits are now mostly vegetated. Nightingales sing there each spring but up here the only constant sounds are those of chirruping grasshoppers and humming bees. I had heard a yellowhammer and a family of greenfinches on the way, and a pair of twittering swallows swooped overhead. The passing gull and feral pigeons were silent.

Burham Down is best known for its wild flowers and associated insects. Today's prize flower

Yellowhammer

was marjoram, the pink clusters standing proud in the sunshine. A hand lens would have been fun for the smaller flowers: eye-bright, fairy flax, thyme, trefoils, agrimony, basil and many others. Their delicate colours, shapes and patterns declared their identity and beauty. I was also struck by the particular beauty of lesser bindweed - certainly not a weed here!

White, blue, brown and orange butterflies flitted, danced or darted about. The Trust has reintroduced the silver-spotted skipper here but I saw none today. Pink and black burnet moths seemed common and I found some of their pointed, tissue-like cocoons on the grass stalks. Hoverflies, honey and bumble bees and orange-coloured soldier beetles graced the tops of hogweed, and a single large, bright blue dragonfly raced through.

Lunch finished, I walked on. That farm animals graze here was confirmed by a water trough. Grazing by ponies, sheep or cattle is part of the

One of the disused chalk pits

management plan: to return parts of the hillside to short-cropped chalk grassland, free of encroaching bramble, hawthorn and blackthorn scrub but rich in wild flowers. Dead stumps of trees cut flush with the ground, areas of rough vegetation cut by hand and a single very neatly tidied-up bonfire site provided further evidence of the Trust's Green Team at work.

A second sign listed some of the many species recorded here and acknowledged the support of government and business in funding the management. "Good," I thought, "Everyone should want to share the cost of the work."

Finding another stile, I entered the ancient woodland, immediately noticing the comparatively cool and dark atmosphere. A family of wrens seemed concerned by my presence as I looked briefly for orchids. The spring flowers had gone to seed and it seemed that only a covering of ivy and dog's mercury remained.

Climbing into the hawthorn, hazel, ash, yew, oak, whitebeam and inevitable sycamore was old

Rockrose

*Chalkhill blue
butterflies*

But there in the bag and all around was glass: whole and broken bottles. Why do people go to such lengths to spoil the countryside? Disappointed, I left it all … perhaps a staff litter-pick one day.

I recalled the saying: "Sometimes I sits and thinks, and sometimes I just sits". With Kent stretched out before you bearing the marks of Man's treatment and mistreatment, this is a great place to sit and contemplate. Maybe, I thought, there should be a sign like the one I remember at the top of Snowdon which says in four languages, 'Wanderer, stop awhile and think of the marvellous works of God and of your short passage on earth'.

Nigel Matthews
KWT Head of Education

man's beard and yet more ivy. There are dormice here, but I decided not to search for the tell-tale holed hazelnuts. The only mammal signs were rabbit droppings and burrows, the latter showing just how close the underlying chalk was to the surface. Doubtless there are squirrels, foxes, badgers, hedgehogs and the usual smaller species, and a visit early or late in the day could be rewarding.

Peering into the branches, I watched a family of long-tailed tits, together with some young yellow-faced blue and great tits - a foretaste, I thought, of the autumn and winter tit flocks which would later roam the woods. I had noticed autumn gentian listed on the sign; the whitebeam was loaded with berries, as yet unripe; dry seed heads of bluebells could be seen beneath the trees … I really must come back at each season of the year.

Returning along the deep-cut path, I climbed up through the twisted yew roots to retrieve a bright blue carrier bag someone had carelessly dropped. I would do my bit to keep the place tidy.

Dropwort

Burham Marsh

THE Kent Wildlife Trust's reserve at Burham Marsh is on the east bank of the Medway between Rochester and Maidstone, close to the villages of Burham and Snodland. The reserve is part of the Holborough to Burham Marshes SSSI, which English Nature has designated principally for its brackish-loving flora and winter wildfowl.

Industrial activities, both past and present dominate this part of the river Medway. Cement workings were the principal industry of the early twentieth century, and the remains of disused factories are still present at Holborough, Burham and Wouldham. The old chalk quarries and clay pits that served the cement industry still show as significant features in the chalk of the North Downs. Cement manufacturing is in recession with Holborough works currently closed but planning to reopen. Paper manufacture is the main industry on the west bank. Our neighbours across the Medway are Snodland Paper Mill, whose pulp and waste paper stacks, on an area of land that forms a horseshoe bend in the river, seem to project intrusively into the reserve. Farther south, Aylesford Newsprint Mill is another cross river neighbour. A newer industrial development on the east bank is Southern Water's Burham Treatment works, which provides drinking water for the people of the Medway towns. Our reserve fits neatly around and between these modern industrial intrusions in the landscape. Any visitor cannot be unaware of the industrial nature of this valley. The reserve however complements and softens the landscape and offers some unique habitats for wildlife, adding considerable contrasting interest to our industrial neighbours.

There are two distinctly different major habitats within this reserve, tidal reed-bed and grazing marsh. The marsh, grazed with cattle by a local farmer, is the less interesting part of the reserve. The tidal reed-beds, although dominated by common reed, are not a mono-culture, and several other very interesting plant species are present. One of these is the marsh mallow, a plant of the highest saltmarsh and occurring on the edges of the river wall. In similar places, another interesting plant, the giant marsh sowthistle occurs. A visit in August should find both of these species in bloom.

The diverse and plentiful bird population is the best known feature of Burham marsh. Virtually every month there is something of interest to see. The winter months of January, February and March are the peak months for the wintering birds. Teal and lapwing are the dominant bird species. Up to a thousand teal are present on the river and grazing marshes, which

Marsh mallow

Bearded tit

Reed warbler

is of national significance being approximately one percent of the teal wintering within the United Kingdom. However these numbers do not occur every winter. Another bird of note in the winter is the water rail, which is more difficult to see, as most of the time they remain hidden in the reed-beds. However on very cold days, particularly when there is snow, they will come out of the reed-beds to feed on the muddy river banks at low tide, offering good views to the patient observer. Other species present during the winter include white-fronted geese, shelduck and the occasional bittern. Birds of prey such as kestrel and sparrowhawk are regularly seen. Winter thrushes, redwing and particularly fieldfare, are often present in the adjacent fields and hawthorn bushes. In the afternoons gulls and cormorants fly over to the river estuary or to the old gravel pit lakes at Leybourne.

High numbers of snipe are present in most years during March indicating their spring migration. The Trust manages part of the reed-bed by cutting reeds early in the winter to create ideal roosting conditions for this species. The much rarer jack snipe is also often present.

Twelve pairs of heron nest in oak trees at the southern end of the reserve, but their nests are well out of sight from the eastern side of the river.

The next event is the return of the spring migrants. The most important bird to reach this area in April is the nightingale. These birds start to sing as soon as they arrive and call at any time of the day or night. The nightingale population of the Burham/New Hythe area is an important stronghold for this species, which, in England, is retreating south eastward in range. Nightingales continue to sing until the beginning of June when their egg hatch occurs. Other birds singing during

Redwing

Teasel in flower

this period are reed warblers which prefer the smaller reed-beds, sedge warblers in reedy thickets and whitethroats preferring the drier hawthorn and bramble areas.

Autumn migration is not so spectacular but there are still birds to see. August will bring migrant waders to the river with common sandpiper and green sandpiper calling from the river bed as they chase one another at low tide. Sand martins and swallows have previously roosted in the reed-bed from any time between mid July and the end of September. When these roosts occur they are quite spectacular with thousands of swirling birds 'beating up' the reed bed as they go to roost. Unfortunately sand martins are not as common as they used to be and these sights of birds coming to roost are rarely seen now. Lapwings return to the grazing marsh in August with numbers building up throughout the autumn. October often brings bearded tits. These small birds can be observed clambering up reed stems and making their distinctive 'pinging' communication call.

Late Autumn is the best time to see the barn owl hunting at dusk over the sea walls or grazing marsh. Its ghostly white shape glides gently just above the ground as it searches for its prey.

Rod Smith
Ornithologist and chairman of KWT Conservation Committee 1991 - 1994

Collingwood

The Great Storm of October 1987 caused extensive damage here. Many specimen trees came crashing down on that fateful night, perhaps the most lamented casualty being a giant sitka spruce - reputed to be the tallest tree in the locality and possibly one of the first of its kind brought back from western America by David Douglas of Douglas fir fame. Many of the scars of the storm have since been softened by nature, but this fallen monolithic spruce tree still dominates the glade it once shaded, its dead branches pointing accusingly at the now benign and peaceful sky.

Years have passed since Herschel's army of gardeners tended this plot. It is now an enchanting gem of a nature reserve, neither large nor high profile, yet therein lies so much of its charm. It is a secluded haven of tranquillity, abounding in delights and surprises for those who tread its paths. Within its modest bounds may be discovered a variety of habitats - lake, ponds, ghylls, glades and mixed woodland, a diversity which encourages a wide range of flora and fauna.

Among the beeches, oaks, chestnuts and hornbeams are to be found wild service trees, an unexpected London plane and bamboo clumps! In the damp and shady water courses feeding the main lake liverworts and ferns flourish; *Osmunda regalis* - the royal fern - being particularly noteworthy. Flowers abound: aromatic wild garlic and ground ivy, bold yellow flags, delicate enchanter's nightshade, sporadic helleborines. In autumn there is a profusion of toadstools: King Alfred's cakes, stinkhorns, puffballs and remarkable brain fungi.

The reserve is one of the most productive sites in the Weald for craneflies, boasting a phenomenal thirty-seven species! Butterflies and

I CAN'T hear any traffic. The air is filled with birdsong and the scent of blossom. Bathed in late May sunshine I am sitting beside the lake in what remains of Sir John Herschel's garden. Sir John Herschel was Astronomer Royal and lived here from 1840 until his death in 1871. It was from the roof of his residence - Collingwood House - that he used his telescopes to discover and carry out extensive observations of double stars and nebulae. In 1843 he observed the Great Comet. His famous father, Sir William, discovered Uranus. Sir John had this lake constructed, and the surrounding six acres landscaped and planted as amenity woodland.

However all that was long ago, and time has changed the face of Collingwood. Now only traces of Herschel's boat house, summer house and rhododendron walks remain. Many of his original exotic plantings have fallen victim to recent storms.

Fox

Puffballs
Lycoperdon pyrforme

moths frequent the glades and pathways. Sightings of rabbits and squirrels are commonplace. Sometimes one may spot a fox on its travels. Grass snakes can be discovered sunning by the path or swimming in the lake edge. Large carp move just below the water's surface. Marsh frogs can surprise with their sudden loud croaking. Diligent searching in hazel clumps may reveal the spherical nest of a dormouse, fashioned from leaves, grass and strips of honeysuckle bark. There are birds aplenty: woodpeckers, nuthatches, tree creepers, owls and a variety of water birds including heron and the occasional kingfisher. At dusk, bats hawk for insects above the lake and in the glades. As darkness falls, glow worms light one's path.

How this wood alters with each season! In spring it is alive, clothed in a backdrop of myriad greens accentuated by drifts of bluebells, comfrey, wild daffodils and primroses. Summer's profuse growth burgeons in, rose bay willow herb bordering the paths to head height, and wayside brambles providing rich pickings of plump berries for the peckish rambler. Lily pads cover almost the entire surface of the lake. In autumn the lilies have died back and the clear waters carry the colourful flotsam of wind blown leaves, the autumnal charms of lakeside trees reflected to perfection. By winter the surface of the lake might be frozen, the cavalier tracks of a marauding fox picked out on the ice by a light dusting of snow.

Let us return to Collingwood's past. At one point Collingwood House became an hotel. Under

Tree creeper

Silverwashed fritillary

this same sky where Herschel gazed at the constellations, literary luminaries such as Agatha Christie and Rider Haggard are said to have boated across the lake. I wish I could travel back to those earlier days. I could walk these grounds with Sir John, noting the young sitka sapling on the edge of the glade. I could watch Miss Christie and Mr. Haggard as, oars dipping, they progress across the glittering waters of the lake . . . But then again, I think that perhaps I am the lucky one. Sad for them that they can't see the reserve as it is today - untamed, secretive, a favoured spot - one of Kent's loveliest wild places.

Lewis Johnson
Honorary Warden

Cowden Pound Pastures

In August, the meadow is blue with devil's-bit scabious

Betony

I T WAS a hot, sunny day in late summer 1990 when I first saw this hidden valley a few miles from the county border near Edenbridge. At the time I was working on a county wide habitat survey and had been walking all day through some visually attractive but botanically uninteresting fields. Notebook entries for most meadows during the survey would take a matter of seconds and one or two lines would describe the variety of plants present, but as I walked through what was later to be the Cowden Pound Reserve it soon became obvious that this was a very special place and would take much longer to describe.

Fighting my way through a thicket of bracken and bramble I came into a small clearing, where small clouds of common blues and meadow brown butterflies were feeding on flowers of bird's foot trefoil and black knapweed. Anthills, standing proud in the middle of the clearing suggested little disturbance for many years, and when more were found amongst the tangle of encroaching bracken and bramble it became clear that this had been an open field in the not too distant past.

Thoughts full of anthills and ancient fields, I pushed my way through a gap into a strip of woodland. Nothing particularly unusual here, but as I emerged from the woodland my recent excitement was soon surpassed as I took in the sight. Another open field sloped away to my left with the most stunning display of a breath-taking

Brimstone butterfly

Whitethroat

and vivid blue. The slope was a carpet of devil's-bit scabious looking like a Monet painting. A closer look revealed betony, eyebright, heath spotted orchid and a host of other plants that I would expect to find in ancient undisturbed grassland.

In yet another field, large ant hills dominated the view as far as the eye could see. Short, well cropped grass with the occasional smattering of yellow from tormentil and fleabane and purple from self heal gave it a completely different character to the first two fields I'd just walked through. Though each one an individual, the three fields were united by a marshy area with an abundance of rushes and sedges made colourful by corn mint, lesser spearwort and ragged robin. Beyond this, a meandering stream cut into clay and sandstone. The exposed rocks and banks of the

Old anthills show that the meadow has never been ploughed

Hazel nuts

Ragged robin

stream were dripping with ferns and mosses and strewn with moss-covered fallen trees.

It was as though I'd just walked on to a piece of land that time had passed by, the valley had escaped the ravages of modern agriculture, pesticides, drainage and fertilisers and had been traditionally managed with occasional grazing by sheep or cows. The roar of a 747 on route to Gatwick brought me abruptly back to the 20th century, as it drowned out the soothing sounds of grasshoppers.

The map I was carrying showed no signs of this area having been given any sort of designation local or national but very shortly after that time the site was visited by Trust staff and designated as a county wildlife site. A few years later, after part of the site was tragically ploughed up, English Nature gave legal protection to the rest of the site by designating it a Site of Special Scientific Interest. A few years after that, the Trust was approached by the owners, the Religious Order of St. Andrews, to lease the site and manage it as a nature reserve.

When I visit the reserve these days it is usually to help cut bracken and bramble or to put up fencing so that we can re-introduce grazing or to talk to visiting groups about the management of the reserve.

At these times I often find myself trotting out the standard description . . .' the reserve covers 14 acres with 9 acres of unimproved grassland, 5 acres of woodland . . .' but when time allows I still try to sit and enjoy the site for what it really is, a beautiful relic of unspoilt Kent countryside.

Dave Hutton
KWT Reserves Officer (west)

Cromers Wood

Wood mouse

The pond at Cromers Wood

CROMERS WOOD is situated 1½ miles south of Sittingbourne in the parishes of Sittingbourne and Tunstall. It is named after the Cromer family who were Lords of the Manor of Tunstall from about 1420 until the death of James Cromer in 1616 when the estate passed through his daughter Christian to the Hales family. The male line of the Hales family ended with the death of the sixth baronet Sir Edward in 1829 and his great niece Mary Hales sold the estate in 22 parts in 1872. Cromers Wood was then bought by Edward Twopeny who owned Woodstock Farm. At the turn of the century Woodstock Farm and Cromers Wood came into the ownership of a Mr. Bensted who in 1946 sold Woodstock to Shell Research. They established a large agricultural research centre there. In 1989 the Kent Wildlife Trust entered into a management agreement with Shell and when Shell closed down in 1996 they generously gave the wood to the Trust in memory of their presence in the area.

The wood covers an area of about 60 acres. At its highest point it is 75 metres above sea level dropping to a height of 50 metres at the southern end of the wood. Lying on the south-east side of a dry dip slope valley variations in soil types contribute to the diversity of the wood's flora and fauna. Botanically the richest part is the slope down into the Highsted valley where the underlying chalk greatly reduces the acidity of the soil. Although now a sweet chestnut coppice, parish records show it is a site of an ancient woodland. Surveys of the woodland flora have recorded 30 species indicative of ancient woodland including wood spurge, butcher's broom, Solomon's seal and herb paris and sheets of bluebells which indicate that the land has been wooded for centuries and may never have been cleared. A further indication that this is part of an ancient woodland lies in the insect fauna. Rare micro-lepidopteran moths characteristic of ancient woodland have been recorded. Cromers, like many woods in south-east England, was planted with sweet chestnut in the 17th and 18th centuries to provide a quick and renewable source of timber for the big estates. When Cromers was planted we are not quite sure. However, the Steward's returns for the Tunstall Estate in 1745 record that in 19 sections of the wood the underwood was cut and sold, so it seems likely that sweet chestnut was planted before then. This is borne out by the size of the large chestnut stools circular in shape and rotted out in the centres indicating that they are very old.

The management plan is to carry on the traditional coppicing. For this purpose the wood has been sectioned off into 19 cants which are cut

Common frog

Sparrow hawk bathing in the pond

in rotation on a 15 year basis. We also plant oak and beech to increase the number of standard trees creating the more attractive coppice with standard habitat. When a cant is coppiced light gets to the woodland floor and woodland flowers thrive creating ideal conditions for insects. As the undergrowth develops blackcaps, chiffchaffs, willow warblers, garden warblers and yellowhammers find a suitable breeding habitat. By the fifth year of growth the chestnut canopy has closed over blocking out the light, the undergrowth dies back and for insects and birds its attractiveness wanes. In view of this it is essential to coppice at least one cant every year to ensure a suitable habitat for breeding birds and insects. The ideal situation is to have cants at every stage of growth from 1 to 15 years at all times.

Rides are also being widened by removing the chestnut stools creating permanent areas for woodland flowers and the associated insects and birds. Instead of burning the lop and top, the twiggy parts of the chestnut are used to make dead hedges which form an ideal habitat for small mammals, hibernating insects and small birds like wrens and dunnocks.

The first project undertaken by the Trust was the cleaning out of an old pond. An excavator was hired in the autumn of 1989 and about a metre of leaf mould that had accumulated over the years was removed and a hide was erected overlooking the pond. Now every spring up to 600 frogs arrive to breed, followed later by toads, and two species of newt. The pond is also a focal point for bird watchers as the nearest other pond is over a mile

Barn owl

Badger

away and in dry weather there is a continual stream of birds coming in to drink and bathe. In one hour on one occasion 26 species of birds were recorded visiting the pond. Over the last three years sparrowhawks have become regular visitors and on occasions three and four have been present at the same time. It also attracts hawfinches, birds which are elusive and not usually easy to see. At dusk in winter woodcock often flight into the pond to bathe and feed and good views of this secretive bird can be obtained. 89 species of birds have so far been recorded on the reserve. 47 of these are regular or occasional breeding species, the rest passage migrants or winter visitors.

Cromers, like most coppiced woodlands, lacks suitable nesting sites for hole nesting species because there are few mature trees. To remedy this, nest boxes have been erected greatly increasing the number of breeding titmice. As willow tits like to excavate their own nest holes in rotting trees some nest boxes are fitted with a block of polystyrene to resemble rotting wood. Tawny owls are now a regular breeding species making use of nest boxes, while before their erection they only used the wood for hunting. All three woodpeckers are present. Green and great spotted regularly breed and the lesser spotted occasionally. Seventeen species of mammals have been recorded on the Reserve. In 1990 a small mammal survey revealed a good population of woodmice, voles and shrews and a larger than expected population of yellow-necked mice. On summer evenings two species of bat, pipistrelle and long-eared can often be seen hunting and bat boxes have been put up for summer roosts. Insect life on the reserve has yet to be studied in detail. Moth trapping evenings which are carried out

about twice a year usually produce 60-70 species; Elephant hawk, poplar hawk and privet hawk have all been recorded. Butterflies are increasing benefiting from the widening of the rides. 21 species have so far been recorded and in 1997 we had the first brown argus and small copper records.

So far 192 species of vascular plants have been found and there are still parts of the wood to be botanically surveyed in detail. Seven orchid species are present, notably lady and birds' nest.

Ted Coleman
Photographer and Honorary Warden

Darland Banks

Fragrant orchids

I N SIMPLY scenic terms, today's visitor to the Reserve could well be forgiven for suppressing something of a shudder: even the green oasis impact is subdued by the weight - and inelegance - of the adjacent urban sprawl. But what of the Banks before the urban sprawl?

I first experienced the Darland Banks late in 1945 (rather a sobering time ago) as a lad, just returned from wartime exile in Australia. Those first solid memories are actually very robust, because the place was really impressive, made the more so by being within a walk or an easy bike ride of my home in Gillingham. As now, the Darland Banks were precipitate dry chalk downland,

broadly southerly to south-westerly in aspect, characterised primarily by long rank grass (even then) and studded, densely in places, with hawthorn scrub.

The view then to the south was of limitless dry chalk valleys with occasional lanes, tracks and farmsteads, capped on the distant skyline by the vast expanse of Lordswood, in the depths of which nestled the small village of Walderslade, ill-served by public transport but great on a bike if you liked hills. Times change! Today to the south, some fields and trees can be seen still, but only by the discerning eye, and even that discerning eye must come to terms with an artificial (and floodlit) dry ski slope.

To the southwest, the immediate impression is of urban sprawl, and not particularly elegant or sympathetic at that, either to the environment or to the inhabitants of the dwellings. Away to the west lies Chatham in all its millennial majesty, with multi-storey car parks and the Octagon Centre dwarfing the green dome of the old Town Hall, and the once dominating Military Road. Further still in the distance, modern development has effectively erased Rochester Castle and Cathedral from the prospect unless you seek the aid of binoculars.

Fifty years ago, the eastern Banks were much more heavily, even commercially, grazed than the western, with many fewer hawthorns. In consequence, to the young naturalist it was the western that appeared more typically chalk downland. Here, among the tall brome grass, grew thyme, salad burnet, knapweed, marjoram, milkweed, horseshoe vetch, kidney vetch and scabious, plus many, many others. Oddities included grass-leaved pea (or crimson vetchling - a personal favourite still), and regular but not common, fragrant, pyramidal and particularly man orchids.

For an orchid-enthusiast youngster this was hard going - Queendown Warren, only a short bike ride away, was vastly superior in numbers and species, and for spectacular drifts of plants like bee orchids the valleys running towards Walderslade were the places to go. No whiff of lizard orchids then - they were spoken of only in hushed tones and to be found only at a 'secret locality' in east Kent.

The butterflies in those childhood memories were dominated by browns and blues - but which? Sadly, for butterflies, memory is not sharp enough, but no difficulty with the moths, for the six spot burnet occurred in what seems, even now, to be droves, crawling all over both vegetation and watcher, whirring away on stridently colourful wings.

Ornithologically, too, the eastern Banks came second to the western. On the western were skylarks in profusion, occasional pairs of meadow pipits, masses of whitethroats as you would expect, and the gems (even in those days) of two or three pairs of red-backed shrikes. Nest finding then carried no stigma, and of all birds red-backed shrikes were among the least secretive as they headed for their homes in the hawthorn. These summer visitors are - rather were - among the most enjoyably watchable of our birds. Beautiful, with fascinating behaviour and a song that comes

Man orchids

and subsequently Coward, not least because the colours were brighter than portrayed, rather than the reverse as you might expect.

So times have changed, but the changes heavily underline the need to maintain areas such as the Darland Banks, lying in close proximity to urban areas. They retain a special status, meriting protection as nature reserves. The pressures to allow housing to overrun them will be high but perhaps less so in such steep terrain as the Darland Banks. The challenges of maintenance may be substantial, but the recompense lies ironically in their very nearness to large numbers of people of all ages. Fifty years ago, the Darland Banks triggered in me interests which were to mould my life. Today, the opportunities offered to inform, to educate and particularly to shape the attitudes of succeeding generations of youngsters to environmental pressures and needs are simply invaluable.

Jim Flegg
Horticulturalist, author and broadcaster

as a pleasant surprise. Tragic that today's young birdwatchers miss this treat.

The eastern Banks were not wholly dead: an aged orchard round the farm buildings in the valley held each year a noisy pair of wrynecks, but the enduring memory is of my first green woodpecker. This would have been in 1946, and regrettably was a road casualty - which did however allow close inspection, and marvelling. I suspect that this was the key that opened the door to a great deal of subsequent birdwatching! To a nine-year old, with powerful images of lyre birds and kookaburras in mind, and familiar in an everyday sense with birds as brilliantly colourful as the rosella parakeets, British birds had not yet made any real impression. The sheer beauty of plumage and the brightness of the colours of the green woodpecker in the hand was unbelievable - and resulted in hours of poring over the Observer's Book of Birds (where wartime austerity reduced many plates to black-and-white)

Dog rose

Denton Bank

Denton bank with early purple orchids

Bugle

Cowslips

top of the scarp slope, alternating from the chalk to the clay with flints, with pockets of acid-loving gorse intruding strangely into the otherwise alkaline flora. The woodland floor is studded with bluebells, with the occasional flash of gold from yellow archangel and pink from red campion. A sparrowhawk shoots low through the hazel coppice, silent and deadly on scarcely moving wings. I muse on the absence of orchids - associating early purple orchids with woodland, yet here they grow in profusion in the meadow.

And then out in the sunlight again . . . Denton Bank is the typical Wildlife Trust reserve. Not big enough to be famous or to boast an international or even a national designation, without the rarities to make it a naturalist's pilgrimage, it has variety, fragility, peacefulness - and in its combination of cowslips and early purple orchids in May, one of the truly great sights of springtime in Kent.

Pete Raine
Director of KWT, 1989 -1998

TIMING a visit to Denton is tricky - there is only one week of the year when the bluebells in the wood are still flowering, matched by the display of cowslips and early purple orchids in the adjoining chalk grassland. It could be early May, or it could be late May - depending on the weather - and it needs to be sunny to get the full effect.

The first view of the pasture is breathtaking. From a distance, the purples and yellows in the meadow are bright enough to be foxgloves and buttercups rather than the orchids and cowslips they really are. Some of the early purple orchids stand eighteen inches high, in clumps of every shade from pale lilac to deep purple. The blue pyramids of bugle run through the grass, while the understated and undistinguished spikes of common twayblade are overshadowed by their more colourful companions.

Leave the chalk grassland and walk back through the woodland. The path zigzags across the

Yellow archangel

Downe Bank

Bluebells in Hangrove Wood

It is interesting to contemplate an entangled bank,
clothed with plants of many kinds,
with birds singing on the bushes,
with various insects flitting about,
and with worms crawling through the damp earth,
and to reflect that these elaborately constructed forms,
so different from each other in so complex a manner,
have all been produced by laws acting around us
Charles Darwin.

Bee orchid

CHARLES DARWIN'S poetic conclusion to *The Origin of Species* may well have been inspired by Downe Bank, which the Darwin family affectionately called "Orchis Bank". Orchids had fascinated Darwin and the relationship between orchids and their insect pollinators provided the subject of his next book.

Charles Darwin spent the last forty years of his life at Down House in Kent. His experiences during the famous voyage of the *Beagle*, especially his observations of the wildlife of the Galapagos Islands, provided strong evidence that living organisms had evolved. The exotic nature of those islands captured the public imagination and Darwin's discoveries have become linked with the Galapagos. However Darwin discovered the mechanism of evolution in the Kent countryside, with his theory that organisms evolved by a process he called natural selection. In his *Autobiography* he recalled 'the very spot in the road, whilst in my carriage, when to my joy the solution occurred to me: and this was long after I had come to Downe'. We can speculate that he might have been travelling along the road from Downe to Cudham, perhaps on a visit to Downe Bank. If Charles Darwin was alive today he would

Slime mould
Physarum leucophaeum

Violets

remind us that clues to life's origins abound in our own countryside. We only need to follow his example and go on hands and knees to share his experience.

When we became wardens of Downe Bank we learned that the late Sir Hedley Atkins, who was curator at Down House at the time, believed that the Kent Trust had bought the wrong place, since orchids grew on the sloping banks of the valley beyond the garden. Whilst that did not detract from the reserve's wildlife interest as an SSSI (it is a fine example of relict chalk downland), it would have significantly decreased its international scientific importance. However he gave permission to research the issue in the library

Tendrils of white bryony

Magpie ink cap *Coprinus picaceus*

and even joined in one morning still wearing his pyjamas. When we had almost given up hope, we found a letter that had been written five years after Darwin's death, it provided conclusive evidence that Downe Bank was indeed "Orchis Bank". Emma Darwin, Charles Darwin's wife wrote to their daughter Henrietta Lichfield reminiscing about their life at Downe and Henrietta noted that ...' Hangrove ... had been one of our favourite walks in the old days - a wood, with hazel undergrowth cut down periodically, and in the hedges gnarled old beeches good for children to climb. On the left of Cudham Lane was a grassy terrace under one of the shaws of old beeches, which we called "Orchis Bank". Here grew bee, fly, musk and butterfly orchises. From this terrace looking across the quiet valley we saw the shingled spire of Cudham church showing above its old yews'. "Orchis Bank" was the Darwin family's name for Downe Bank, in those days it was called Rough Pell. Bernard Darwin had described Hangrove as a charming little hanging wood, with a slippery, sloping path through it, which led to Orchis Bank . . .' It is a dear little platform of turf, one of the few bits of genuine, close-cropped, chalky, down turf left, with a typical shaw at its back'. Visitors to Downe Bank still slip and slide down the same path and enjoy the same views.

Charles Darwin died more than 100 years ago. His ideas caused great controversy but he is now regarded as one of the world's greatest thinkers.

Plants provided him with the weight of evidence for his theories. We realized as we began to look at Downe Bank through his eyes, that many of the plants which he studied were local wild plants that still grow there. In a short essay that Darwin wrote describing the scenery, he might well have been describing Downe Bank as we know it today . . . ' The first period of vegetation, and the banks are clothed with pale blue violets to an extent I have never seen equalled and with primroses. A few days later some of the copses were beautifully enlivened by goldilocks, wood anemones and a white stitchwort. Again, subsequently, large areas were brilliantly blue with bluebells'.

Wild orchids are the main attraction for visitors to Downe Bank. Their elaborate pollination mechanisms gave Darwin evidence for descent with modification. He considered that our native bee orchid and pyramidal orchid were two of the most important subjects he had ever studied. Our common primrose, the cowslip and their hybrid the false oxlip, provided important clues to solve his question - what is a species? The hopfields and hedgerows of Kent provided further evidence of evolution. Climbing plants, such as our wild bryonies and wild clematis have special adaptations to enable them to compete with other plants. Darwin's special genius found inspiration in small and familiar things.

As wardens, working with volunteers from the Green Team to conserve this special site, we have become acutely aware of the continual struggle for existence. As Darwin so aptly wrote . . . 'It is difficult to believe in the dreadful but quiet war of organic beings going on in the peaceful woods and smiling fields'. Darwin would have been fascinated by the many natural events that have affected the countryside since his death. During the lifetime of

Pyramidal orchid

White letter hairstreak

the reserve we have experienced the scrubbing up of downland and waves of myxomatosis, (nowadays an exploding rabbit population is devouring our orchids). Dutch Elm disease brought down large elm trees and their loss threatened our population of the endangered white letter hairstreak butterfly. The 1987 storm completely flattened one large woodland area. Invasions of alien plants and animals, such as the sycamore and grey squirrel compete with native species. Threats of global warming remind us that constant change is a feature of our environment, organisms are continually adapting to survive.

As we celebrate our fortieth anniversary we can claim that Kent was the birthplace of the science of ecology: Darwin's vision has led us to the Rio biodiversity initiatives. We feel privileged to be wardens of this reserve and to have known all its wardens, especially Frank Brightman, who persuaded the Trust to make Downe Bank their first freehold purchase.

John and Irene Palmer
Photographers and Honorary Wardens

East Blean Wood

East Blean Wood with cow-wheat

THE Kent Wildlife Trust's involvement with East Blean Wood is essentially a story of the successful rescue of one of the rarest and most threatened butterflies in the British Isles - the heath fritillary. The butterfly with its intricate chequered pattern of orange and brown upper wings and lattice of yellow, orange and brown undersides, enjoyed a wide distribution across the southern counties of England prior to World War Two. The modern recipe of agricultural intensification and abandonment of uneconomic woodlands was largely responsible for the fritillary's drastic decline. The butterfly's current distribution is reduced to a collection of isolated pockets in the south-west, a couple of re-introduced populations in Essex and some colonies in the Blean Woods.

East Blean is part of the extensive block of ancient woodland which forms a green mantle to the north of Canterbury. Because of the woodland's great age it supports a rich diversity of species, many with highly specialised ecological requirements and thus vulnerable to environmental change.

The Kent Wildlife Trust bought the wood in 1987 to establish a nature reserve the primary aim of which was to bring the heath fritillary back from the brink of extinction. Surveys that year indicated that the population in the wood was down to a few hundred individuals hanging on in a handful of scattered locations. The plan was simple; to re-establish an annual programme of autumn - winter coppice cutting along traditional lines to produce a regular supply of cow-wheat upon which the caterpillar of the heath fritillary is dependent. To ensure that the fritillaries could find the new carpets of cow-wheat a network of open rides maintained on shorter coppice cutting regimes ranging from two to ten years has been developed to encourage the butterflies to venture along them and use them for breeding too. After a decade of this management the heath fritillary population on our reserve is now counted in thousands.

This cycle of management also supports many other butterflies as well as moths and dragonflies during the early years after cutting. Birds such as the nightingale use the regenerating young coppice in its fourth to eighth year after which warblers and dormice take over as the canopy closes over.

The great American biologist Edward Wilson elegantly summarised the concept. "The natural dynamism raises the diversity of life by means of local destruction and regeneration". On relatively small isolated nature reserves we intervene to perpetuate patterns of natural cycles albeit on a humble scale.

John McAllister
KWT Reserves Officer (east)

Underside of heath fritillary

Heath fritillary

The Gill

Bugle

Broad buckler fern

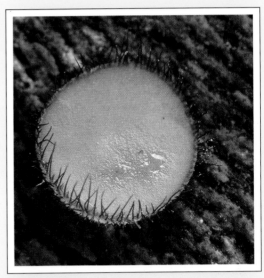

Eyelash fungus *Scutellinia scutellata*

THE WAY in to the Gill is not prepossessing, a rusty farm gate, a concrete stand and a grass track along the edge of a field, but then there is a choice to go into the reserve itself along the old lime avenue track or further along enter down a mossy, bumpy slope to the pool track. It is a ghyll here, a steep sided valley, with a stream at the bottom. As elsewhere in the reserve the slopes are coppice chestnut with some oak and other standards with a lattice of birch. The spectacular avenue of limes suffered in the storm of 1987, a few down completely, others losing huge branches. The bank by the limes is a sun trap so the drift of snowdrops flowers earlier than in the gardens. The bugle which follows is a miniature forest of rich blue spikes and bronzed leaves. As the summer arrives the ground is baked so the flush of mixed fungi which appear here in autumn must be sufficiently well buried to find the moisture

to grow. One evening we heard the cheeping of young in a nest in one of the trees and waiting quietly were able to see the greater spotted woodpecker come to the hole. That evening too we heard a garden warbler, it was perching in the grove of aspen trees which has grown up on the bank. There are plenty of wild rhododendrons along the valley, in spite of the saw and slash of the working teams anxious to rid an English wood of this invasive foreigner.

The grassy bank is a continuing delight. In winter the bumps are bright with a golden green moss. In the spring the violets appear so the leaves cover the ground and the soft purple flowers abound. Later in the year great patches of common speedwell cover the slope with dense spikes of pale blue flowers. We have been lucky enough to see a slow worm and a coiled grass snake sunning themselves here. One rather chilly evening we set up a moth trap on the bank, a box of cardboard egg cartons for the moths to rest on away from the singeing light. These large moths have splendid names: common marbled carpet, clouded drab, scalloped hazel, peach blossom, shuttle-shaped dart were just a few we found.

The winter rains raise the pool level until it overflows trickling down a gully to the stream. A log which acts as a bridge for the gully also acts as a larder for the badger which scrapes the bark away to find tasty larvae. The eyelash fungus grows on it as well so that the minute orange saucers with their fringe of black eyelashes can be found in the autumn.

Some scallops have been cut along the stream track, exposing the honeysuckle entwined branches and some piles of mossy logs. New piles of logs now provide homes for insects and fungi to grow. The ground here is carpeted with wood anemone in the spring and an invasion of foxgloves has taken place promising a spectacular show of flowers later in the year. There are violet helleborines nearby. On the opposite bank the ferns are luxurious. Hard fern, just vegetative in the winter will send up the special spore bearing fronds later starting up another cycle. The male fern, buckler fern and lady fern, also growing along the banks, have much larger divided fronds.

Along by the marsh where the stream fans out a cleared area awaits new arrivals. An old stump was a regular site for the bitter boletus fungus but it has dried out now and it is unlikely to reappear for a while. The stream here becomes choked with large bitter-cress, the flowers have delicate white petals and purple anthers. With lady`s smock and hairy bitter-cress this makes the third of the *Cardamine* genus of flowers in the reserve.

Grass snake

Yellow pimpernel

At the corner of the two parts of the L shaped reserve the badgers have their main set. I have yet to see them come out but I have seen all other signs of their presence. The freshly excavated earth outside the holes, the old bedding dragged out, the well trodden path down to the stream and the dung pits, some indicating a badger of no mean size. There are several holes showing occupancy at different times around the edge of one of the quarries where clay was presumably once removed. This is now a black marsh with tussocks of pendulous sedge though in the spring there are patches of kingcups which make golden splashes in the gloom. Walking along the edge track towards the badgers corner there is a magnificent view to the north, across fields and cottages to the ridge of Linton and the North Downs 15 miles or so away.

But on a hot day one can plunge into the cool of the woods once again to the alder coppice where stands the lone pine. The slope here faces north, the coppice has grown fast from the bare stools so is shading out the rich growth of lesser spearwort and yellow pimpernel which carpeted the damp slope.

The Gill was given to the Trust by the Franklin family. There are no public footpaths and access is difficult. However visitors will experience a sense of quiet tranquillity and isolation that is increasingly hard to find in this part of the world.

Jean Lea
Honorary Warden

Ham Fen

wetland

THE Ham Fen reserve covers some 30 hectares of fen, fen carr and meadows on peat, lying in a valley in the low chalk plateau which shelves gently down from the high chalk downs to the south-west, to the alluvial marshes south of the Isle of Thanet.

Ham Fen has been known to naturalists for a long time. It was formerly known as "Ham Ponds" or "Ham Brooks". The earliest reference to its plants that I have been able to trace dates from 1805, in the "Botanist's Guide through England and Wales" by D. Turner and L.W. Dillwyn. In this book the fen orchid and the marsh helleborine are recorded there, together with several sedges, including the saw sedge, flat sedge and few-flowered spike-rush. M.H. Cowell published a book "Floral Guide to East Kent", in 1839, which gives quite detailed lists of species to be found then at "Ham Brooks", most of which, except for the fen orchid, were still to be found there into the early years of this century. We know however that the fen orchid was correctly recorded, as there is (or was) an ancient Kent specimen in the Herbarium of the University of Edinburgh.

I have known Ham Fen for over 50 years myself. I saw it become drier and more overgrown with scrub in the 'fifties and 'sixties, so that the marsh helleborine, still there in 1955, disappeared. The creeping willow, plentiful when I first knew the fen, was not seen again after the flooding with sea

Codlins and cream

water that occurred in the great storm of 1953. Red rattle survived until 1954 but has not been seen again. Least bur-reed survives in nearby Worth Minnis. Ham Fen, however, remains a unique place for Kent and south-east England. The nearest habitats of similar type are now in those fens of East Anglia that have survived both drainage and also the more insidious lowering of the water tables due to extraction from boreholes.

There are now no longer any relict lakes as there were last century. But it is remarkable what are still present of the interesting fen plants formerly known here, and, still more encouraging,

Scarlet tiger moth

Tussock sedge

what species have already reappeared with the Trust's management work.

Of the orchids, marsh helleborine has not yet re-appeared since c.1955, but southern marsh orchid is locally common, together with leopard-spotted marsh orchid, which is locally a feature in some years. Marsh fragrant orchid was here until c.1930, but the site is too overgrown now for this; though it could be re-introduced.

The saw-sedge, formerly dominant over much of the fen, became very reduced in the 'fifties and 'sixties as the fen became overgrown, but now that much clearance of competing vegetation has been undertaken, it is showing an excellent recovery. The only other south-eastern English site for it is at Dungeness.

The marsh fern is greatly increasing now among reeds and tussock sedge also. Bared or

Broad bodied chaser dragonfly

bank, as has happened in some East Anglian sites. The fen is entomologically very rich - one of its most notable moths is the very local scarlet tiger.

We hope that, over the years, most of the former species which seem to be absent at present, will re-appear. Ham Fen is a fascinating place.

Francis Rose
Botanist and author

excavated areas of peat have encouraged a welcome reappearance of bog pimpernel, brookweed, lesser water-plantain, and small sedges such as long-stalked yellow-sedge but several other rare sedges formerly here, such as flea sedge and lesser tussock sedge have not yet reappeared. Tufted sedge is still here.

The dykes have very interesting aquatic vegetation, with several pondweeds, of which fen pondweed, now only known here east of Somerset, and south of the Thames, is still flourishing locally.

The meadows to the south-east are not yet part of the reserve but were rich in fen meadow species into the 'fifties, and with management many of these may well reappear from the buried seed

Southern marsh orchid

Hewitts Chalk Bank

The bank with evening primrose

Dark mullein

OVER one hundred years ago men building a railway from London to Sevenoaks and beyond came to Hewitts. There they found a hill and as railway trains cannot go over hills they had to make a tunnel and to make a tunnel they first dug a deep cutting. Someone must have asked "Where are we going to put all the spoil"? And somebody said "Up there". And so the men, sweating, struggling and swearing wheeled barrows of chalk up to the top and emptied their barrows. As more and more barrows were emptied so the pile of chalk - chalk that had not seen the light of day since dinosaurs roamed the land - stretched out like a peninsula jutting out into the ocean.

In later Victorian times men wanted somewhere to dump their rubbish and other men said "Dump it there". Later yet other men asked if they could build a golf course and they were told that they could. They did not need the land with piles of chalk and piles of rubbish and sought to give it away. Other people who understood that nature could cure industrial scars accepted it. Now wild plants grow on the chalk and birds and butterflies come to the flowers and insects find homes where once there was rubbish.

And so the men who dug and the men who dumped bequeathed to people they never knew a nature reserve where mulleins, evening primroses, marjoram, thyme, basil, orchids, goats rue, felwort, violets, milkwort, flax, yarrow, agrimony, yellow-wort, ploughman's spikenard and more than a hundred and fifty other plants prosper and create a patchwork carpet of colour both in spring and summer.

John Hodge
Honorary Warden

Toadflax

Basil

Holborough Marsh

Yellow flag iris

ONE of the great pleasures (and there are many) of being Director-General of The Wildlife Trusts is being able to spend half a day in the middle of the week wandering around a nature reserve and call it work. Friends tease me by saying my whole life is a holiday. I always deny it hotly, but I have to admit there are times when they are not far wrong.

My half-day at Holborough Marshes was a case in point. It was a Thursday morning in late January, a beautiful sunny day, crisp but not cold, perfect for being out and about. To show me around were Pete Raine, Director of the Kent Wildlife Trust and always entertaining company, and Dave Hutton, reserves officer for the Trust and a mine of fascinating information on Holborough and other reserves managed by the Trust.

Pete had asked me to visit Holborough and then write about my impressions. I was glad to do so because I had been to Holborough once before in late summer and because it is in many ways a typical Wildlife Trust nature reserve with the same problems and challenges that many of our reserves face all over the country.

Holborough is a lovely place, a wonderful mixture of grassland, scrub, hedges, ditches, fen, tidal mud and reedbed on the west bank of the River Medway with chalk downland across the river valley to the north and Blue Circle industrial workings to the south. Some of the 2,300 Wildlife Trust nature reserves in Britain are stunning. Skomer, Cley, Bradfield Wood or the island of Eigg are very special by any definition. However, the great majority of our reserves are relatively small, relatively unspoiled remnants of a vastly changed surrounding landscape. Sixty years ago most of our reserves would have been nothing special because they would have been little different to vast areas

Gypsywort

Lapwing

of our countryside, and they are only special now because so much else has been destroyed.

Holborough is a bit like that. There are no spectacular national rarities, no unique examples of some highly threatened habitat, and no extraordinary abundance or variety of animals or plants. But it is a very pleasant place with quite enough interesting features to justify being a nature reserve – and an SSSI too. There are good water vole populations along the ditches. What's so special about that, you say? Nothing except that water voles are the fastest declining mammal in Britain, thanks primarily to predation by American mink, and are in serious danger of extinction in many parts of the country. In January, we put up several snipe on the meadows. Nothing special about that either except that snipe populations are also plummeting at a terrifying rate because so many traditional wet meadows are drying up. Indeed, the day I was at Holborough we put a sluice board in one of the ditches to raise the water level on the meadows to make them a better habitat for birds. Just two days later, 16 mallard, 17 teal, 40 lapwing, 1 redshank, 6 snipe, 100 rooks, 1000 gulls, 30 goldfinches, 40 pied wagtails, and 30 meadow pipits were counted – a far greater abundance of birds than the day I was there.

Plants like marsh mallow, bladderwort and opposite-leaved pondweed can all be found at Holborough – and all of them are much rarer than they once were. Nightingales breed in the wooded scrub, bearded tits overwinter in the reedbeds, and marsh harriers and peregrines are regular winter visitors.

So what else makes Holborough a typical Wildlife Trust nature reserve? Its size (85 acres), its proximity to people (half a mile from Snodland) and its land tenure (owned by Blue Circle and on

Nightingale

the River Medway and looks down directly on to the reserve, the Trust is concerned that too many visitors could cause disturbance problems. If the site was bigger, it would be easier to keep one part for visitors and the other visitor-free.

Holborough's proximity to, and ownership by, Blue Circle also makes it typical. A great many of our nature reserves are parts of larger areas of land that were acquired for industrial development, but for one reason or another those parts were not developed and were then leased or given to the local Wildlife Trust to manage. These kinds of arrangements have their disadvantages in that our tenure on the land is often not as long-term as we would like (which can make it difficult to secure funds, for example from the lottery, for management work). But they have advantages too. They force us to work with literally hundreds of companies around Britain whose everyday activities affect wildlife and the environment. This often gives us a good opportunity to influence these companies, not just in relation to how we manage their land as nature reserves but to their environmental performance more generally.

So, enjoy your visit to Holborough. It's a lovely haven in a fairly heavily industrialised landscape, and by supporting the work of the Kent Wildlife Trust you can make sure it stays that way.

Simon Lyster
Director General of the Wildlife Trusts

a 15 year lease to the Kent Wildlife Trust) are all features with which I am familiar. Eighty five acres is about average for a Wildlife Trust nature reserve yet much, much smaller than, say, the average RSPB reserve. The relatively small size, especially when combined with proximity to lots of people, brings lots of challenges. The biggest of these is to meet the twin objectives of maximising the value of the reserve for wildlife and for human visitors. Too many people and you risk excessive disturbance that could be damaging, especially in a small site. Keep people out and you waste a valuable opportunity to get local people interested in, and supportive of, the wildlife on their doorstep. A balance has to be struck. At Holborough there are a number of dog-walkers and local visitors. As the main path is up on the sea wall along the banks of

Hothfield Common

Bog cotton at Hothfield Common

Keeled skimmer dragonfly

I SPENT three of the most formative years of my life in Kent, being taught to kill things. I emerged in the summer of '69 with a degree in horticulture, a sizeable repertoire as a folk singer, and, I'm ashamed to say, a deep dislike of Hothfield Common.

As a Yorkshireman in exile, I was astonished by Kent. Nothing had prepared me for the autumn smells of ripening fruit and hops. I saw my first glow-worm, heard my first nightingale, and spent hours sketching primroses, wild orchids and old man's beard. Kent opened my eyes to softer, prettier more melodious versions of the wildlife I had grown up with in the gritstone valleys of Sheffield and the Dark Peak - but Hothfield Common was a blot on my mental landscape.

Most of my academic studies revolved around agro-economies and pesticides - pretty heavy going. Even my half unit in floriculture (flower growing) concentrated on ways of wiping out the creatures that might reduce the value of carnation crops. I was taught chemistry by the man who proudly claimed to have invented DDT, and the term 'organic' was exclusively applied to evil-smelling chemicals with lots of Cs and Hs in their molecular make-up. The nearest we came to mushrooms and toadstools was an earnest study of life-threatening fungal diseases - nothing about the role that fungi play in the wider scheme of things, as the ultimate recycling agents, or as delicious ingredients in the best risottos.

Hothfield Common should have provided the natural break from the chemical warfare of the killing fields. This was the place where students were taken, to learn the principles of ecology, of natural plant communities, and the intimate link between wild plants and animals, soils and local climate. To be fair, I must have learned something. Years later, I dredged up memories of quadrats and transects, of soil profiles and botanical keys when tackling landscape projects in the Saudi Arabian desert, and again when building a convincing case for wildflower meadow management in inner-city parks. Sadly, though, there was nothing in my Hothfield Common memory bank which suggested that this might have been an interesting, or beautiful, or precious place.

In fact, of course, this nature reserve is all those things, but you need to spend time in its silence, watching the mist rise through a pink dawn, or enjoying the yaffle of a resident green woodpecker, in order to appreciate it. You need to have a really close encounter with the plants and animals that manage to make a living in the wet acid soils, to see the splendour of the wildlife. You need to be told about the link between the relative rarity of peat bog communities, and their exploitation for peat-based compost and grow-bags, to understand why Hothfield Common is a nature reserve worth fighting for. Nothing in my horticultural education ever made the link between peat and the wonderland of sundew, bladderwort, bog asphodel, slow-worms and heather.

The bogs and lowland heaths of Britain really are special - our equivalent of the rainforest when it comes to global responsibility. I admit that they aren't glamorous. Their beauty rarely takes your breath away, and the species which live there are more honestly labelled 'interesting' than awesome or spectacular - but these are some of the rarest, most endangered habitats in the world. In Britain, we have the lion's share of them, and in Kent, Hothfield Common is the sole surviving example. What a good job it is in such capable hands. Historically, the heath was much more extensive than it is now - no doubt a wild, forbidding place, a barrier to travel, and a haunt of highwaymen. Indeed, the Lord Mayor of London was once robbed of everything but one stocking and his shirt on Hothfield Common, and the Highwayman responsible, Robert the Wizard, was later caught and hanged in chains outside a nearby hostelry.

The open nature of the heath has changed, as oak and birch woods have seeded in and colonised the boundaries. Indeed, the heath and bog had all but disappeared before the Kent Wildlife Trust took on the management, and started beating back the trees and letting in the light. Now, thanks to skilful cropping, stump removal, mowing and grazing with cattle and goats, the glorious purple flowering heather is returning, and the sunlight can reach the surfaces of the bogs and ponds which occupy the hollows. Wetland wildflowers which had not been seen for decades have miraculously re-emerged, and the reserve is alive with insects.

Heather

It is the wetness of the valleys which makes Hothfield Common particularly valuable for wildlife - indeed, our student name for it was always 'Hothfield Bog'. No peat is dug for horticulture here, but the gardening public do still pose a threat to this important habitat. The water which flows from the Downs to feed the wetlands has been drying up and the great increase in garden hose-pipes and sprinklers is at least in part to blame. In recent years I have recalled my long-forgotten horticultural education in order to campaign for wiser use of water in our gardens, so perhaps in revisiting Hothfield Common after 30 years, I've finally squared the circle. I now realise that Hothfield did have an influence on my subsequent

Orb spider
Aranius quadratus

Cross leaved heath

career, because I've used what horticultural and ecological skills I have to celebrate the moods and the magic of nature much more than the science and statistics.

For Hothfield Common to survive, there needs to be a popular concern for wild, wet places, and there needs to be a better understanding of the link between the nature on which we depend, and the nature of the way we live. The secret of survival for the slow-worms and grass snakes, the sundew, bog asphodel and cotton grass, the rare dragonflies and moths, and Hothfield Common's whole community of wildlife, is wiser use of water by the gardeners of Kent, linked with continuing support for habitat care by the Kent Wildlife Trust. There is a much tougher challenge, too - to coax the present generation of students out of bed in the early morning. That way there's just a chance that they may catch the morning mist, soak up the silence, and store up some life-long memories of the true magic of Hothfield Bog.

Chris Baines
Professor of landscape architecture,
author and broadcaster

Hunstead Wood

OWNERS of the Macmillan Guide to Britain's Nature Reserves will read that" Hunstead's steep sloping beech woodland falls to a stream and pond". Most of the beech trees did just that sometime in the early hours of October 16th 1987. I probably mourn their loss more than most but the wood is still alive and will doubtless develop over the next hundred years into a beech hanger as majestic as the one I miss.

The deep ditch on the northern edge is one of Hunstead's oldest features and is all that remains of the pale which once kept the deer within the confines of the forest. Chartham Hatch, the nearby village, was the location of a gate or hatch, where entry could be made into the forest. The earliest record of the wood's name is from 1535 when it appears as "Hounsted", meaning "the place where hounds are kept" from the Old English "Hund stede", giving us a clear picture of this edge of the forest perhaps up until the time of the Reformation.

There is a pond in the corner of the wood with wood horsetail by its margins and Solomon's seal nearby. When winters were still enjoyable I

Chaffinch

Penny bun fungus *Boletus edulis*

remember skating there while a blood red sun sent lengthening shadows horizontally through the beech trees. Large depressions in the side of the storm damaged beech hanger nearby may have been where brick earth was dug. The coppice there would have been put into service to produce charcoal to fire the local oast and to provide the large number of hop poles employed at that time - two or three to each hill.

The bog, or valley mire, a very rare habitat in Kent has a moody atmosphere all of its own. On late summer evenings, fingers of mist crawl over moisture-laden boggy hollows and dark peaty pools. Its carpet of sphagnum moss is home to myriad species which are dependent on this specialist acid habitat. Sphagnum was collected here and was used as a wound dressing both for stemming the flow of blood and for aiding the healing process with its antiseptic properties.

Whenever I find it necessary to walk down memory lane Hunstead is never far from my thoughts.

Neil Morris
Warden of Hothfield Common

Fly agaric fungus
Amanita muscaria

Ivy Hatch

Skunk cabbage

IVY HATCH is, at a mere 2.2 acres, our smallest nature reserve and was given to us in 1975 by Mrs. Robertson. Most of the people who have heard about this reserve know that it harbours a flamboyant exotic cuckoo in its semi-natural nest. In fact, skunk cabbage, a garden pond plant that has spread from the streamsides through half of the reserve, has done a gross disservice to Ivy Hatch. Not only is it an alien, but also it is of lurid hue and rampantly successful! It has proved very difficult to control and made the reserve seem slightly ridiculous.

The wetness of Ivy Hatch is a delight in such a dry county, and that alone is justification for its inclusion in our portfolio. It is particularly charming at bluebell time when it reminds me of the woods and streams of my childhood in Buckinghamshire. There is a lovely blend of the tamed and the exciting in the various constituents of the area. Often we overlook the miraculous in the commonplace, like the wonderful symmetry of the unfurling fern frond, the beauty of an individual bluebell flower, the crunch of dead leaves. Ivy Hatch offers so much to engage the senses - even the colour of skunk cabbage is stunning.

In the main, we look to acquire bigger reserves these days, and though we have little chance to expand Ivy Hatch, it still has an intrinsic value, not least by giving us a window to an historic past. We often refer to our Nature Reserves as "Jewels in our Crown". Although Ivy Hatch isn't the diamond that is Lydden, nor the emerald that is Marden Meadow, to me Ivy Hatch is a small cabochon ruby, a little gem.

Vicky Golding
Chairman of the KWT Conservation Committee
from 1994 to 1996

Marsh marigold

Kemsing Down

Green hairstreak butterfly

THIS is a genuine local nature reserve located on the steep slopes of the North Downs looking across the gault valley towards the greensand ridge, once fully wooded, with an ancient trackway leading across the valley.

The ancient woodland was cleared by early settlers and grazed into the 19th Century by sheep. In their absence the scrub and trees continually try to reoccupy the slopes. Only rabbits and the frequent attention of volunteers keep open some areas of chalk grassland with its rich diversity of plants and insects.

White helleborine

Chalk milkwort

The site was purchased by the Parish Council in 1976 which then invited the Kent Wildlife Trust to become involved to assist with management advice and organisation of working parties to support the work of local people.

In my early days as Chief Executive of the Trust I worked at weekends with the various Green Teams to meet the volunteers and to see some of the reserves. I well remember Kemsing Down. On two visits we cleared scrub - the usual and inevitable task on the chalk downland. My sweat and thorn punctured hands were added to those of others. Each year the task programme is largely

Field maple leaves and fruits

the same - an eternal battle against the invading trees and shrubs.

If sometimes we ask ourselves "Is it all worth it?" then we should take a walk over Kemsing Downs in late May, as I did this year. Emerge from shrubby corridors into those open grassy areas - see the carpet of wild flowers about to burst into life - see the many man orchids which occupy the lower slopes - the brilliant blue of the milkwort - and watch the clouds of butterflies moving over the short grassland.

A rough recording on Whitehill Down showed more than 65 small heath, 30 common blue, 20 dingy skippers and 2 grizzled skippers,

5 male brimstones and one female - which kept teasing me as I tried to take a photograph, moving a few feet each time as I focused the camera. The highlight was undoubtedly an enjoyable sequence of my further photographic attempts on a green hairstreak - so dark in flight - so beautifully green when it settles and shows those brilliant underwings. While I was busy I was hurdled by joggers and passed by walkers along the North Downs Way with benign smiles - we were all having a great time.

Summer brings the busiest time for plant, insect and animal life but it is during the spring and

Sloes

autumn that the soft colours of the trees and shrubs are particularly beautiful.

I wander through the quiet shady woodland of Shorehill with warblers and woodpeckers, thrushes and tits, and then into another open area - where it is a similar story, clouds of butterflies, the promise of chalk flowers and in the margins white helleborine and twayblade. That is why it is all worth so much effort in the winter months to keep those areas open.

We have to admire the foresight of Kemsing Parish Council and those local people who had the vision to safeguard this delightful section of the Downs. That is why it is important for the Trust to continue their support of local action. A classic example of the very best in wildlife conservation - the affection and enthusiasm of local people, combined with the expertise and commitment of the Kent Wildlife Trust and hopefully an object lesson for many other parishes and local societies.

Fred Booth
Chief Executive of KWT from 1982 to 1987

Kiln Wood

Common spotted orchids at Kiln Wood

CERTAIN smells evoke childhood. The herbal fragrance of spring rain on a hedgerow full of cow parsley, white nettle and violets reminds me of that time, as does hawthorn and rowan blossom on a day positively humming with heat.

All these thoughts filled my mind - the sights, sounds and smells of my past, as I set off on my first visit to Kiln Wood, just north of Lenham. I was in search of one of Kent's most exquisite treasures. On a perfect day its fragrance and hue is matchless. I had come to Kiln Wood for the bluebells.

April 1998 was one of the wettest on record. It was blowing a chill north-easterly as I set out to meet my guide, Fred Booth. Suitably dressed in clodhoppers, waterproof coat and bobble-hat I thought of a thousand places I'd rather be. My first impression as we entered the site from the southern corner was how intrusive were the sounds of modern living. The roar of the M20 less than a mile away, a nearby railway line, both carrying thousands of folk, oblivious to the wealth of wildlife I was about to discover.

The ground was heavy and wet underfoot, plentiful with that good marsh plant tussock sedge, but where were the bluebells? We followed the deep rutted path. The dank mounds bore small mosses and the distinctive little herb paris. Close by, a chiffchaff, undeterred by the unseasonable weather, sang a merry note. Kiln Wood has a mix

Rosebay willowherb

Common spotted orchid

woodland flowers were emerging, early purple orchids, just one of the orchid species to be found at Kiln Wood, and that true sign of ancient woodland, the yellow archangel.

We arrived at a pond, which must be an important watering place for birds and animals during high summer, its banks thick with water violets and reed mace. Instantly I was transported back to another time and place, pond dipping at Brooksend, probing among the water weed and algae for tadpoles, water boatmen and snails. Here at Kiln Wood, the bright yellow flowers of the marsh marigold bobbed about in the breeze all round the water's edge. Indeed we could trace a small stream simply by following the golden heads meandering back through the wood. This is one of two sites in Kent that you'll find bogbean. We saw evidence of a badger's toilet. Grass snakes and lizards can be found basking near the pond on hot summer days.

of deciduous trees, oak, ash, hornbeam. An abundance of wood anemones meant that the bluebells were not far away. Now the ground flora became rich and interesting - coppicing had created vital space on the woodland floor.

Woodland rides have been opened up by the Trust. The mistlethrush is doing well here, and we saw numerous green woodpeckers. As we made our way to the northern corner of the woods we came upon swathes of bluebells. I confess disappointment - the harsh weather had not been kind to them, their lovely heads closed tightly against the chill. But in their midst other varieties of

Common spotted orchid

Herb Paris

We left the pond and headed round the outskirts of the wood. Trees lay where they fell providing valuable habitat for insects. The dark, dank boggy conditions were perfect too for a variety of fungi, witness a dryads saddle growing as big as a tractor seat. We stepped over the stream, marsh marigolds gave way to twayblade orchids, their pale green flowers just beginning to emerge. Common spotted orchids also flower here.

Common twayblade

Dryad's saddle fungus
Polyporus squamosus

Suddenly it was time to leave. I'd quite forgotten how cold and wet my feet and hands were, having been totally immersed in all there was to see. Did Kiln Wood deliver what I'd expected? Truthfully - no it offered so much more. The wood is a good example of management by the Trust which has produced an environment of great importance to conservation and education.

And the bluebells? There have been better years and richer carpets, but just as I was leaving I caught the faintest whiff of their exotic, unique and thankfully protected fragrance.

Barbara Sturgeon
Radio Kent broadcaster

Lydden Down
National Nature Reserve

Small scabious in August

I hear it said yon land is poor
In spite of all those rich cowslips there
And all the singing larks it shoots
To heaven from the cowslips' roots.
But I, with eyes that beauty find,
And music ever in my mind,
Feed my thoughts well upon that grass
Which starves the horse, the ox and ass . . .
W. H. Davies, Cowslips and Larks

Hoverfly

OF ALL THE damaging environmental effects of modern agricultural intensification, the ploughing or fertilisation of Davies' poor, unproductive grasslands has arguably caused the greatest loss of wildlife. Kent is fortunate in retaining a good representation of chalk downland, but mostly now as small relict patches which give little idea of the majesty of the greensward which once rolled over much of the Kentish hills. Only in a few places, especially in the valleys running into Dover, are there still big, continuous tracts of downland turf, and of these Lydden and Temple Ewell Downs are the finest. They stretch for almost two miles over coombe and spur on the south facing slope of the dry upper Dour Valley, bounded by cropland and woodland on the more fertile soils above and below the scarp. With prospects of grassland and grazing animals all around, it is not difficult to imagine what these valleys must once have been like, with folds below ready to receive the stock for the night; so wonderfully recorded by Samuel Palmer in his pictures of the Darent Valley, where, sadly, little of the old downland now survives.

The Downs then were not marginal to productive agriculture as they are now. Before crop rotations, before legumes, before guano from Peru and long before synthetic nitrogen, the great imperative in farming was to maintain the fertility of the croplands. This was achieved by robbing the Downs (and heaths) of their fertility by folding stock onto the fallows in the valleys, there to dung. The short, springy thyme-scented turf of the Downs and their great floristic and entomological diversity is a direct legacy of the infertility brought about by this old farming system. If fertility is allowed to build up, then a few vigorous species, which can exploit it, mostly rank grasses such as tor

Autumn lady's tresses

Squinancywort

simulates) are in constraining dominant species like the beech and allowing others to survive.

The fascinating variety of the grassland at Lydden almost certainly reflects differing past management regimes as well as the different soils at the top and foot of the scarp. There are plenty of tightly grazed grasslands still left on the Downs, but they are not species-rich downland like Lydden because their fertility has been increased to improve production. This has happened at the eastern end of the reserve where fields were under the plough between 1978 and 1980, then reseeded back to grass before becoming a part of the reserve. They have recovered remarkably; recolonised by many of the commoner downland herbs, but still belied by a more weedy sward which contrasts with the much more species-rich sward of tor grass in the unploughed paddock between them where bee and pyramidal orchids

grass, soon overgrow, outcompete and exclude most of the smaller, slow-growing herbs and grasses of the sward, paving the way for scrub and tree colonisation. Left unmanaged, downland, like nearly all the north-west European lowlands, would end up as a virtual monoculture of the most efficient competitor around, which is the beech tree. A stand of woodland on the reserve reminds us of what this would be like, and its more species-rich clearings, caused by the great storm of October 1987 demonstrate how important such natural disturbances (which management

Adonis blue butterfly

abound. This sward is very different from the next most westerly field which is dominated by yellow oat grass and contains some extensive flowery patches of thyme and mouse-ear hawkweed almost devoid of grass. Further up the valley tor grass and, on the more acid soils above the scarp, gorse, are both potentially invasive species to be watched. For it is here that the more open patches contain some of the richest, old turf with masses of fragrant orchids and, in one special place, that great rarity, occurring only on the shortest of swards - the burnt tip orchid. These sunny patches of tightly grazed turf are also the favoured location of the horseshoe vetch and the adonis and chalk hill blue butterflies whose caterpillars feed exclusively on it. The plant and the butterflies soon go if the rank grass closes in. This has happened at other Kent downland sites and the thriving populations at Lydden have been used as a source of individuals successfully to re-establish populations elsewhere once a short sward has been restored and the food plant re-established. Some butterflies, however, like the longer grass, marbled whites for example as do other insects, notably the great green bush cricket. The recently reintroduced wartbiter cricket prefers rank tussocks in a short sward. Skylarks nest in the long grass and birds such as linnets and yellowhammers in the gorse.

Management of the reserve must thus ensure that all these types of habitat are continuously present. As they are in a dynamic relationship with one another, manipulating the grazing regime - its season, intensity, type of stock - is not easy. In particular, the daily outfield-infield system which was practised in the past is now virtually impossible to undertake, for it is not part of modern farming. Luckily stock mainly dung in limited areas, especially at the top or at the foot of slopes where the soils are already more fertile. Paddocks help by making it possible to rotate the grazing to rest areas whilst orchids are in flower and seed, or even for longer periods. Wonderful displays of flowering sometimes result after a few years continuous hard grazing followed by a rest period. Happily stock keeping farmers still survive in the Lydden area and graze the reserve under licence with cattle. In other places it is more difficult to find graziers who are prepared to use 'that grass which starves the horse, the ox and ass . . .'. The crisis in the livestock industry caused by BSE may make it even more difficult in the future. Increased nitrogen in rain, now in some places up to ten times the previous level before agricultural, industrial and vehicle pollution, may also make management more difficult. In the Netherlands where the pollution is worse, they fear greatly for the future of their chalk grasslands.

As part of both a complex of grasslands in the Dover area and a chain of reserves managed by Kent Wildlife Trust, Lydden is helping to pioneer some of the approaches which may be the key to the long term future of these grasslands.

Silver spotted skipper

Conservation everywhere is moving away from a site-oriented strategy to one which looks at conservation, or sustainable use, of whole landscapes, involving local farming and commercial enterprise and local people. The White Cliffs Countryside Management Project, in which the Trust has been a founder partner, has been greatly successful in doing this in the Dover/Folkestone area. It has restored many of the rank chalk grasslands by re-introducing grazing and worked very effectively with schools and community

Wartbiter cricket

Burnt tip orchid

groups to harness their enthusiasms and energies. Like many of the abandoned areas it has restored, it is sad to see the beautiful Lydden Valley marred at the moment by a landfill operation at the foot of the reserve, just where the sheepfolds once probably lay. Slowly however government money is being switched from supporting excess food production to providing for environmentally friendly farming in schemes such as Countryside Stewardship, which is being employed at Lydden, and generally very effectively exploited to improve damaged environments. Could we see that land as sheepfold once again as part of an integrated system of sustainable land use which achieves both the production of food and biodiversity? Lydden reserve demonstrates the potential for downland restoration. The powers of recovery of natural systems, given appropriate, active management, are not to be underestimated.

'I like to look at the winding side of a great down, with two or three numerous flocks of sheep on it, belonging to different farms; and to see, lower down, the folds, in the fields, ready to receive them for the night . . . the sheep principally manure the land. This is to be done by folding . . .'

William Cobbett, Rural Rides 1830.

Bryn Green
Professor of Countryside Management at Wye College

Marden Meadow

Marden Meadow with green winged orchids in May

SPENT some of my more formative ecological years in Hertfordshire, where we were fairly smug about our portfolio of orchids. Populations were relatively small but the common species were well represented. When I moved to Kent in 1977, I was soon to realise that where Hertfordshire merely has some orchids, Kent has orchid riches in profusion.

Organising a visit to see one of the jewels of nature conservation in Kent usually requires extensive planning, the constitution of an ox and at least a degree qualification in Ordnance Survey six-figure map reading. Enthusiasts have been known to spend entire days, covering many kilometres, searching for an elusive bee orchid or man orchid on a Kent Trust reserve. At Marden Meadow in May and June there are no such problems, for there will be thousands of green winged orchids and it will be difficult to avoid treading on them. The reserve is accessible, flat, and utterly stress-free. Park outside, pop over the stile, and you are instantly transported back to the flower rich fields of the 1930s.

The Trust bought the two meadows and ponds in 1983 from the Executors of George Holliday, a farmer whose father and grandfather before him had farmed the Stone Pit and Holders Farms in Marden. They were traditional small mixed farms which grew hops, a range of apple varieties, a small amount of arable crops and grazing for their dairy herd. The Holliday dairy supplied milk and dairy products to Marden and the surrounding villages.

The meadow in high summer with oxeye daisies and buttercups

Adderstongue fern

Colour variations in the green winged orchids

received no artificial inputs and the very minimum of mechanical treatment.

Their existence as a very special pair of flower rich meadows was a poorly kept secret in the area, and it was regularly visited by interested individuals and groups, including the children of Marden Primary School who introduced me to the place.

Perhaps the two most important species in the reserve are the green winged orchid and its completely unrelated but very close associate, the adders tongue fern. The green winged is really a very modest little orchid, with nothing of the opulent splendour of the lady orchid or the delicate floral complexity of the lizard. What the green winged orchid has is sheer quantity. In terms of its distribution, it is recorded in every Vice-County South of Hadrian's Wall save East Devon and Montgomery. Whilst sympathising with anything trying to thrive around Dartmoor, I suspect that the lack of a record in Montgomery says more about the distribution of the recorders than it does about the distribution of the orchid.

Because of the sheer size of their populations, colour variation in green winged orchids is extensive. Although the majority of the flowers are a breathtakingly deep purple with the characteristic green stripes, a small proportion, usually one to two percent, vary from pale lilac through pink to white. As the flowers develop, it is ironic but amusing to see the tracks leading to the freaks - the pale versions of the green winged orchid so much revered and so extensively photographed.

Although the orchids are the main attraction, the other flowering plants of the traditional hay meadow are present in profusion, but a little later. The orchid phase in May and June exists in a relatively low sward together with the diminutive adders tongue fern. It is succeeded by a much

Mr Holliday was still farming in his eighties, in much the same way as his forebears.

The two fields at Marden Meadow were outliers, about a mile from the main holding and buildings, which may well be the reason for their survival as damp unimproved meadowland. Local wisdom is that the land was far too wet to grow arable crops, unsuitable for growing apples and too far from the farm to be worth growing anything other than grass.

A late cut of hay was taken each year and carted to Stone Pit Farm, where it was stored in ricks and provided winter cattle feed. In return, apart from a limited amount of dung applied occasionally, and a light harrowing, the fields

The pond with water violets

Banded demoiselle damselfly

Dyer's greenweed

higher sward of grasses and flowering plants and develops from a predominantly purple sward to one of pale green grass flowers and white ox-eye daisies. Hay rattle, knapweed and fleabane are common, and the eastern margin has several large areas of dyers' greenweed.

The Marden Meadows are a survivor of a literal bygone age. A thriving sward of modest little orchids living in harmony with other meadow grasses, herbs and ferns, and defying the Common Agricultural Policy. They are the charming remnant of a redundant farming age when the pace was literally "walking", punctuated at hourly intervals by the incongruous incursion of Eurostar trying to cut five minutes off the journey time from London to Paris or Brussels. An idyllic Paradise.

Peter Payne
Honorary Warden

Oare Marshes

"Hello, I'd like to speak to John Gooders.

"Speaking".

"Oh! I thought I'd get your secretary".

"I'm sorry, but she's popped down to the butcher's to get a bit of scrag end for supper" I explained, hoping that this down-to-earth approach would ring true for this mystery inquirer.

"I'm from TVS" the voice explained. "We'd like you to open the Oare Marshes Nature Reserve for us". Wow! Fame at last, and a new, highly lucrative career opening supermarkets and shopping malls, not to mention nature reserves, loomed large. Forget the scrag end . . . bring on the fillet mignon. "We won't be able to pay a fee, but we could run to a pint of Shepherd Neame and your petrol". Great.

Thus it was that I found myself addressing the Mayor of Sittingbourne ("Call me Mr. Mayor" she said), serried ranks of Kent naturalist bigwigs, a TVS news team and an assortment of local birders. And so, to an audience of thousands, could have been millions, I explained that North Kent had always held a special place in my soul and that "The Full North Kent Gear" that we all wore at the time involved every jersey, waterproofs over jeans, a parka salvaged by Millets from the US Airforce that weighed a hundred weight, multiple pairs of serious socks, mittens and twenty-four hours supply of Kendall Mint Cake.

Actually, I felt a bit of a fraud because although I had cut my ornitho-teeth, as it were in North Kent, the Oare Marshes lie on the southern shore of the Swale whereas my old stomping ground had

Short eared owl

been across the channel around Harty Ferry and along the coast at Cliffe, Halstow and Yantlett Creek. Memory fails me, but I cannot for the life of me ever remember taking the Harty Ferry across the Swale to the Oare Marshes. So I presume the ferry was already consigned to history back in the 1960's, which was a pity because half the birds flushed headed straight in that direction.

As a wheel-less tyro, I arrived by train at Kingsferry, walked for miles along the marshland walls and just caught the last train back to London on what became a sort of birdwatchers' special. We would exchange news, see each other off,

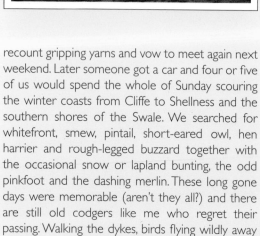

recount gripping yarns and vow to meet again next weekend. Later someone got a car and four or five of us would spend the whole of Sunday scouring the winter coasts from Cliffe to Shellness and the southern shores of the Swale. We searched for whitefront, smew, pintail, short-eared owl, hen harrier and rough-legged buzzard together with the occasional snow or lapland bunting, the odd pinkfoot and the dashing merlin. These long gone days were memorable (aren't they all?) and there are still old codgers like me who regret their passing. Walking the dykes, birds flying wildly away as one approached, their identification being quick and distant or missed for ever, is a sharp contrast

to the hide-bound critical examinations possible of today. Expertise was built up rapidly, but we doubtless missed birds that a feather by feather analysis would have revealed. So we saw no more than the occasional pectoral or white-rumped sandpiper, not so much as a single icterine or melodious warbler, and red-necked and long-toed stints had not even been invented. In rarity terms it was the Stone Age. We kept our records in notebooks rather than on PCs, and the "Grapevine" was the nearest approach to Hotlines and Pagers. Oh! The romance of recollected youth.

And so, as my audience leaned forward in a fever of anticipation (or were they falling asleep), I cut the white tape to tumultuous applause (or was it just relief) and declared The Oare Marshes Reserve of the Kent Wildlife Trust duly opened. Within minutes the bigwigs had whipped me off to

Pintail

Avocet

a local hostelry for the promised pint and, as the first gulp slipped gratefully down, I daydreamed once more about how things had changed.

Sadness and regret were tempered with reality. The wild marshlands could not have survived without the help of conservation bodies like the Kent Wildlife Trust. And it is not just farmers and developers who create problems. The birding boom has turned the passion of a few into the hobby of the multitude and, incidentally, into a multi-million pound business. Quite frankly, the North Kent marshes could never have survived the onslaught of a thousand birdwatchers a day without concentrating them into well-managed nature reserves. The Whitefronts were flighty enough when only a few of us walked their marshes. With hordes of birders they would quite simply have flown away. Harriers and falcons,

buntings and larks would all doubtless have disappeared along with them. And so, when push comes to shove, reserves like the Oare Marshes are as important for the birds as they are for their watchers. They may eliminate that sense of wilderness that we used to enjoy. They may, by bringing us eyeball to eyeball with birds, change identification criteria from jizz to an anatomical analysis. But while we regret these losses we have gained an intimacy with the wildest of birds that was previously impossible. The birds are grateful too and they show it by their presence in increasing numbers. What's more, the full North Kent Gear is no longer necessary and Millets seems to have disappeared from the High Street.

John Gooders
Ornithologist, author and broadcaster

Orlestone Forest

Small copper butterfly

FIRST went to Orlestone as a boy in 1959, after meeting Dr Scott, a well known local lepidopterist, who told me that this was the place to go to see the Duke of Burgundy butterfly. Unfortunately, by then, it was either very rare or extinct, and I did not see any.

Nevertheless all the woodland fritillaries, except the heath fritillary, were there - but sadly by the 1980s all had disappeared.

Much of the pristine forest had been converted to alien softwoods which on the night of 15/16 October 1987 were more or less completely destroyed. Over ninety percent of them were blown over, their roots having been damaged in the heavy weald clay by alternating flood and drought. However, the native oaks which still grew in the Kent Trust reserves within the forest, in Longrope and Burnt Oak Woods, and also along some of the ride margins, stood firm albeit in a rather tattered condition, with broken limbs hanging down or hurled to the ground. In many parts of the forest natural regeneration is being allowed to take its course so that it is likely that it will, in time, return to some semblance of its former glory.

The rides, managed by Trust staff and volunteers, are now full of plants that attract a wide variety of butterflies such as common blue, brown argus and dingy and grizzled skipper with ever-increasing numbers of white admiral whose caterpillars feed on the large tangles of honeysuckle. Single specimens of rare species such as purple emperor and large tortoiseshell seen recently suggest that even if the range of species has changed and some have been lost, others may be moving in. The forest is still an exceptional site for woodland butterflies.

White admiral butterfly

Many rare and unusual moth species are still to be found in Orlestone, attracting lepidopterists from all over the country. Over three hundred species have been recorded in a single July night - a total unlikely to be exceeded in many places in Britain. Amongst them, were such splendidly named Orlestone specialities as the triangle, sub-angled wave, clay fan-foot, scarce merveille du jour, broad-bordered bee hawk and feathered beauty. The last species, ironically, is a recent arrival in Britain, which breeds at Orlestone on the very conifers that we so deplore.

Orlestone Forest, thanks to all those who have helped to reverse some of the decline it has suffered, remains a very special area for woodland butterflies and moths.

Mike Enfield
Reserves Officer (east) with KWT from 1984 to 1989

Broad bordered bee hawk moth

Park Gate Down

WE JOINED the Trust in the early sixties and although not active members at the time we were sufficiently interested in wildlife to subscribe to this comparatively new venture.

Moving to the Folkestone area from the Medway Towns in 1968 we came under the guidance of Tony Wilson the sole conservation officer in East Kent at that time who operated from his Canterbury home. We volunteered for the one and only working party and after a suitable period of probation were asked to be wardens at Park Gate in 1977. Our brief then was to walk around the reserve and keep an eye on the stock fence, and to keep the visitors from entering a

Eyebright

Late spider orchid

small fenced off area. On this unremarkable patch of grass Hector Wilks had chosen to broadcast some monkey orchid seeds obtained from the plants at Ospringe in 1958.

Although records state that the first flower was recorded in 1965, the orchids were not really established until the seventies. After two plants were dug up in 1982 a high fence commonly known as the monkey cage was erected with a padlocked gate, making access limited to when the wardens were present. It was evident that interest in conservation was growing by the large numbers who came to see them. This fence was removed in 1986.

Park Gate is important not only for the monkey orchids but for twelve other orchid species, some of which only appear occasionally. The tiny musk and the late spider cause great excitement as do our other rarities, the slender bedstraw and aquilegia. During the flowering season our phone is busy and calls come from all over the country. Most visitors from far away stay

Monkey orchids

Springtime bank

locally overnight and "do" other chalk downland reserves in the area. Camera buffs armed with the latest equipment take endless pains to get the perfect shot. We marvel too at the various methods used to shield specimens from the wind, always a hazard at Park Gate. Whereas a body lying prone might be useful to deflect the breeze, over the years many ingenious screens using metal, plastic and glass have evolved.

It is always a thrill for us to visit on a winter's day and climb the slope to the main monkey area above the chalk pit. We walk slowly up and down ready to spot the first rosettes which are netted to protect them from rabbits.

In spring experts visit to measure and record numbers. Until very recently propagation in laboratory conditions was difficult, but experiments at Kew have recently proved more successful.

Summer brings a profusion of colourful chalk downland flowers many of which are the food plants for a variety of butterflies. To walk through the reserve on a hot summer's day and encounter clouds of these lovely insects is an experience. Later still the grasses with their graceful moving stems have a different appeal. Despite its small size, Park Gate has an all-year round attraction for visitors.

Cattle are used to maintain the sward at the right height. These are put on at certain times of

Primrose

False oxlip

the year and do a very good job keeping the reserve in pristine condition. The ant hills, an important feature, stand out well after grazing has finished.

Other vital help is given by volunteer working parties on Wednesdays and Sundays throughout the autumn and winter months. Only very severe weather is allowed to jeopardise the programme of scrub control, bracken bashing and fencing. Whatever the elements throw at them, the regulars arrive, suitably attired, complete with sandwich boxes and flasks. Sometimes jacket potatoes in foil are baked in the bonfire and raked out as required - delicious on a cold damp day.

Great camaraderie exists within the group. We are also grateful to those members who volunteer to spend a morning or afternoon on the reserve, meeting visitors and showing them round, during the busy flowering season.

We feel privileged to have been wardens for twenty-one years. During that time we have increased our knowledge and made many friends. We hope we have helped to enthuse others and foster their interest in Park Gate's particular attractions.

Helen and Keith Hudson
Honorary Wardens

Parsonage Wood

PARSONAGE WOOD, was acquired in 1965 as a generous gift from Captain Collingwood Ingram, a then resident of Benenden and a noted ornithologist and horticulturist. I had the pleasure of meeting him once back in the 1970s when despite being a little frail and in his late nineties, he insisted on walking across the orchard and around the wood so that he could show us the chequer tree.

Parsonage Wood is one of the Trust's oldest freehold reserves, only the original Lydden Temple Ewell reserve and Yockletts Bank can claim seniority. Arguably it is also one of the most attractively situated of the Trust's reserves

Early purple orchid

being set in a pattern of undulating small scale meadows and copses with long distance views of rolling countryside. It is still the second largest wealden woodland reserve and although at 24 acres not very extensive, it has all the essential elements of a good wildlife area. A wide range of native deciduous trees and shrubs, deep streams (ghylls), ponds and a very long woodland edge, make it like an island set in a sea of farmland. The boundaries of the wood have hardly changed in the last hundred years and probably for much longer than that. Similarly, the surrounding countryside appears to have escaped major alteration, the immediate landscape remains small scale meadowland with hedgerows and copses. This continuity and variety of habitats are undoubtedly good for wildlife and this is one of the reasons why the wood was selected as a Site of Special Scientific Interest in 1981.

Although the wood does not now enjoy an access track of its own it must once have been on a highway because there is an ancient track which just touches its western boundary. Now no more than a footpath this is still known as Twysden Lane and still retains remnants of ancient banks on both sides with old coppice stools of hornbeam and a good variety of shrubby species. The wood too is classed as being of 'ancient' origin. That is, it has been continuously wooded for many centuries although the individual trees may be of no great age. The largest oaks were probably only planted towards the end of the last century. One or two of the remaining beeches, huge trees on the ghyll edges could be around 150 years old and some of the hornbeam coppice stools could conceivably be older. Butchers broom, woodland hawthorn, chequer tree and pendulous sedge all occur here in varying amounts and are sure signs of the antiquity of the wood.

The landform of the wood is probably what will strike visitors with its main plateau dissected by a series of narrow ghylls descending from west to east to a depth of around 30 feet. The water which feeds the ghylls either arises in the wood, seemingly imperceptibly from almost permanently moist flushes or as run off from higher ground to the north of the wood. Except in the very dry summers of the 1990's a small flow is maintained throughout the year making a very modest contribution to the River Rother which the stream joins near Rye.

'The very depth of the ghyll, the continuous flow of water and the canopy of trees overhead all help to maintain ideal conditions for ferns, mosses and liverworts and these are one of the most important features of the wood'. Or so I wrote in 1985. Two years later in October 1987 came the unforgettable storm which tore the canopy from over the main ghyll. Fortunately many of the uprooted trees fell over it and many continued to grow! So now, nearly eleven years on, the devastation is hidden by what looks like young woodland. Much of it is in fact vertical stems growing from horizontal trunks still several feet off the ground, and the moss and fern population still flourishes. Of the 71 different mosses recorded the most important species occur in the ghylls, for example *Hookeria lucens,* a moss which is rare in the south east. Colonies of ferns are also a feature of the ghylls for example:- hard fern (an indicator of very acid soils) hay scented buckler fern (rare in Kent) as well as broad and narrow buckler ferns. A walk through the deepest part of the ghylls is not recommended for the faint-hearted with its sudden changes of levels, slippery rocks and

White bluebell

predatory brambles. However in the shallower upper regions of the ghylls springtime colonies of golden saxifrage can be viewed with no effort from the footpath and, as with most woods, this is the time for the most spectacular display of wildflowers. Bluebells - the white variety is a particular feature - wood anemone, bugle primrose and so on, all hurrying to bloom before the tree canopy shades them out.

Excessive shade was very evident when the Trust took over the management of the wood. Most of the wood is of coppice origin but coppicing had lapsed in the preceding forty years. So the policy has been to undertake cutting of small areas of coppice to create a mosaic of light and shade throughout the wood. This will be a continuing management policy, along with opening up of glades along the rides and clearing around the ponds to encourage a greater variety of plants

Hay scented fern

Spotted flycatcher

and their associated wildlife. This gradual opening up of the wood has already increased the number and the variety of butterflies and dragonflies to be seen on the reserve. Mainly they are common species like speckled wood butterflies and common darter dragonflies. That is perhaps the fascination of any wood, you never know what will turn up and transform the dullest walk in the worst weather by a chance discovery of for example: a group of purple helleborines, a hobby feeding young (which only happened once!) a newly emerged broad bodied chaser, or a great grey slug (a resident still, I hope, down in the ghylls). If the

expectation ceases it is time to put away the field guides and retire to an armchair.

Parsonage Wood is a place of many moods and infinite fascination. A visit here will never disappoint.

Mike Wilson
Honorary Warden

•

Polhill
Bank

I HAVE known Polhill for almost thirty years. The bank was a favourite place for family picnics and for children to play roly-poly. Snowy winter visits were good for sledging and it became part of our traditional Boxing Day walk by way of Meenfield Woods and Shoreham village. I remember it as open grassland with chalk herbs and many orchids including bee, pyramidal, fragrant, common spotted and man. Large swathes of rock rose and birds foot trefoil were festooned with common dodder. Scattered along the slopes were sweet briar roses with occasional wayfaring tree, spindle and common hawthorn.

Rabbits kept the scrub at bay at the north-western end where the rare Kentish milkwort could be found hanging onto the bare chalk above the entrance to the railway tunnel. I used to visit the steep cutting dressed in a hard hat and orange jacket accompanied by a British Rail official armed with a whistle which he blew to warn me of approaching trains. I hope that this small insignificant rare plant still manages to cling on there.

The magnificent tall mature beech trees above the bank with their low hanging branches made excellent swings and climbing frames for small children .The deep beech litter beneath was ideal for white helleborines and birds nest orchids. These trees were felled by the Great Storm of 1987 .The wind swept along the wooded slopes and brought down most of the trees. The slopes are now a tangle of dead wood, bramble, chalk shrubs and young beech under which, to my great delight, the two uncommon, chalk loving Amanitas (*A. solitaria* and *A. strobiliformis*) can be found.

.Since the Trust took over the management in 1992 the bank is returning to its old form. Scrub has been cleared and sheep graze the bank in the winter and in the summer the grassland blooms. It is an excellent place to see butterflies and many common species such as meadow brown, brown argus and common blue can be abundant. Grizzled and dingy skippers are also present in May and one can often see a fast flying dark green fritillary zipping along the bank as well as such day flying moths as the burnet companion, chimney sweep, and chalk carpet .

Polhill is a place of happy memories of friends, of flowers and fungi, of birds and butterflies and of splendid views of the Darenth valley's patchwork of fields and small woods.

Joyce Pitt
Botanist and Honorary Warden

Hawthorn berries

Mating common blue butterflies

Fungus *Amanita strobiliformis*

Queendown Warren

Summer flowers

A WARM sunny day in mid-August. No measurable rain so far this month. Although the recent weather has been unusually hot, the plants and butterflies seem to be coping well. With every step, meadow browns fly up before us and we see bright chalkhill blues fluttering over the flowers of scabious, burnet-saxifrage and knapweed. Basking on the track in front of us is the first painted lady of the summer. The yellow papery cocoon of a burnet moth is seen to be empty and we see one flying in its usual unhurried manner.

For over forty years we have been coming at this time of year to look for the last downland orchid to flower - the tiny autumn lady's tresses. We are out of luck this time but are confident that they will appear after the next rain comes.

Rabbits have been here for hundreds of years and were introduced into Britain as a valuable source of meat and fur. The poor soil on the chalky slopes of the main bank meant that it was never considered worth ploughing, and this factor has contributed greatly to the specialised flora of the bank. In the history of Queendown the word 'warren' was first mentioned in 1621. The recorded history goes back to 1273, when the widow of Henry III, Queen Eleanor, granted 'to God and the Hospital of Saint Katherine at London without the Tower of London' all her lands 'in Ranham and Hertelepe in the County of Kent and at Roede in the County of Hertford' (Queencourt, Queendown and Queenbury). The name 'Quenedowne' is mentioned in a survey carried out during the reign of Henry VIII.

Sweet briar rose

Broomrape *Orobanche minor*

Early spider orchid

The west bank was known as the 'Stumbles' meaning poor woodland.

Queendown Warren suffered greatly from the Great Storm of October 1987. Potter's Wood, which borders the road at the top of the down, was devastated. It had been a favourite walk. Yellow bird's-nest grew in the shade of the great beech trees. Bird's-nest orchids were often found nearby as were butterfly orchids. In late summer we would find broad-leaved helleborines under the trees and in autumn a wide variety of fungi, including the curious earth star. We arrived the morning after the storm to find the lane blocked by fallen trees. The wood had almost disappeared. This morning, eleven years later, we again walked similar paths in what is a new wood.

Most of the beeches have gone. We could still see the old remains, now covered by brambles. Young trees of other species have taken their place. Once again we can start searching for the plants we used to find there.

Those of us who were involved in the very earliest years of the Trust are an important link with the past. Who else remembers the one time the lizard orchid flowered on the main bank? Or the martagon lily? There are other rarities of which the meadow clary is one. It has large attractive, sage-like flowers that tend to disappear before they set seed. However the plants appear year

Meadow clary

Painted lady butterfly

A Tribute

Queendown Warren was a favourite site of my dearest friend John Knight whose loss I still mourn. He was a founder member of the charity, Plantlife. He was there when I officially opened the reserve in June 1995. Johnny loved to drop names to impress me, such as yellow wort, sainfoin, chalk milkwort and squinancy wort. Horseshoe vetch, though not terribly exciting to look at, is the food plant of the caterpillars of both the chalkhill blue and the Adonis blue butterflies. If the flora is right then the insects are right and if the insects are there then the birds are there too - the green woodpecker being one of the happy inhabitants. In these treasures Johnny took immense pleasure, spending most of his life trying to ensure these places would remain available to us all.

Lorraine Chase
Actress & plant lover

after year. We saw the characteristic leaves of several this morning. The reserve has many other attractions. On our walk this morning green woodpeckers and their fledged young constantly uttered their laughing calls while a chiffchaff quietly chiffchaffed from nearby bushes and a stock dove cooed from a distant tree. On a fine spring day this year we listened to two nightingales singing beautifully in the scrub on the west bank. All this so very close to the busy Medway towns and the hum of the traffic on the M2 motorway.

Owen & Phyl Davis
Botanists

Reculver Country Park

THE twin towers of St Mary's Church are a distinctive feature of the north Kent coast. They can be seen for miles around, guiding visitors as they have guided sailors through the centuries. When you leave the Thanet Way and travel down narrow Reculver Lane to find yourself looking up at them, there is a very real sense of arrival.

People have settled here since at least the days of the Iron Age when a farmstead is known to have existed on the site. Hand-axes from before the Stone Age have been found in Bishopstone Cliffs. The small hill on which the church was built has seen many changes, and clues to its varied past can still be found. Inside the walls of the third century Roman Fort, the first of the line of Saxon Shore Forts to be built, are the remains of one of the oldest churches in the country, founded by the Saxons in the seventh century. The towers added by the Normans in the twelfth century still stand, as do parts of the Parish Church which was gradually extended in succeeding centuries. A romantic ruin, much loved by the Victorians and Edwardians, it still draws many thousands of visitors each year. More about its varied history, together with the strange story of deliberate destruction by its own parishioners, can be found in the Visitors Centre to the west of the car park, whilst a series of snapshots of its history are represented in the mural on the east wall of the Centre.

The church however is only one of the many attractions which makes Reculver such a fascinating place. The beach and Bishopstone Cliffs to the west are one of the few sections of coastline in Kent unprotected by coastal engineers from the sea's attack. The importance of such an unspoiled

Eider

Fringed water lily

stretch of land, with its long history of occupation, its unique geology and its importance to wildlife was recognised by Canterbury City Council, and in the late 1980's a 37 hectare band of land running westwards from just east of Reculver Towers towards Herne Bay was designated a Country Park. Most of the park is an SSSI, mainly for its geological interest, and is also a Local Nature Reserve. The majority of the land is owned by CCC and Reculver Towers is an ancient monument owned by English Heritage. The Visitor's Centre is a focal point of the park for which the Kent Wildlife Trust provided text and illustrations to interpret the wildlife and geology of the Park. CCC provided material on the history and coastal engineering. Kent Wildlife Trust co-ordinated the production of all the displays.

The Country Park and Visitor's Centre was opened in June 1989 by the Duchess of Kent and continues to be developed by a partnership of Canterbury City Council, English Heritage and Kent Wildlife Trust. The main function of a Country Park is to promote informal recreation, encourage nature conservation, and to provide some form of education. Here too confidence can be gained by those not yet ready to venture into wider and wilder countryside. Reculver Country Park fulfils all of these criteria.

From its opening, Kent Wildlife Trust managed the Centre, initially the provision of events through the year for the general public as well as educational visits for organised groups came within the remit of the Centre Manager. Since 1994, thanks to increased funding by CCC, a Warden has been employed by KWT, and school visits are now so popular that there is a Reculver Education Officer. Members of the Friends of Reculver Country Park and other volunteers support tasks in the Park and give help at events and in the Centre.

Reculver has many faces, and its different moods appeal to a wide range of visitors. For casual visitors there is ample space for picnicking, strolling along the promenade and cliff-top, or just relaxing

Hornwrack
Flustra foliacea

on the beach or grass. Most are surprised when visiting the centre to learn how much there is to be seen, and many return with friends and relations to explore further. There are several short walks in the area. The Saxon Shore Way passes through it and Reculver is the starting point for all the Wantsum walks. An increasing number of cyclists come this way, and Reculver's inclusion in the St. Augustine's trail for cyclists and cars has brought it to the notice of still more. Some prefer to come when there are few visitors, appreciating the tranquillity and open space. A walk along the beach to Bishopstone at low tide, returning along the cliff is particularly rewarding, offering wonderful views eastwards across the Wantsum Channel which once divided mainland Kent from the Isle of Thanet.

There is a wealth of wildlife to be found in the Country Park, and for specialists and others who want to explore more widely there is a variety of different habitats. The cliff-top grassland is home to many butterflies and is also a favourite spot for the sand-martins which nest in the cliff-face below. Visitors can explore the ever-changing world of the sea-shore and visit the attractive woodland glen at Bishopstone. Around 150 bird species are seen regularly, some breeding, others spending the winter near the shore where food is plentiful. Autumn is a particularly rewarding time for birdwatchers, when large numbers of migrants pass through. The cliffs we see today are made up of layers of sands and clays left by seas which covered this part of Britain 50 - 60 million years ago and are of particular interest to geologists. Fossils of sea-creatures washed from certain layers can be discovered on the beach at low tide.

Facing due north, with no land between the shore and the north pole for shelter, this coastline bears the full brunt of winds and waves. The rate at which the soft rocks are eroded is indicated by the fact that the Roman fort, built nearly 2,000 years ago, was then almost a mile inland. Attempts to limit damage caused by the sea as seen at each end of the Park, demonstrate different methods that have been used through the years. The defences in front of the Towers were first erected in 1809 by Trinity House in order to preserve them as a day-time navigation marker for shipping. The description in the Centre of coastal management is not only of great interest to many casual visitors, but also the most popular subject of study for senior students.

Reculver is unique not only for all it offers to those interested in wildlife, archaeology, history, or geology, as well as just enjoying the open air and scenery, but also in portraying the way in which both people and nature have played their part in shaping the landscape we see today.

Shirley Thompson
KWT Education officer

Sandwich Bay

Shingle at Sandwich Bay with viper's bugloss

I WAS - and probably still am - the president of Sandwich Bay Bird Observatory. To be honest, I'm not exactly sure how it came about. It was years ago when I was invited to take on this prestigious title, presumably in order to "raise the profile" - and possibly the funding - of the "Obs". I hope my name helped, but I certainly can't take any credit at all for the fact that the Observatory is still flourishing and indeed apparently goes from strength to strength. I say "apparently" because the sad truth is I very rarely get down to Sandwich Bay these days. More ironical still, I am not even sure I'd

ever been there when I was first offered the presidency. Naturally, I felt I really ought to go and have a look. So I did. I well remember my first impression: "this place is really weird"!

It still is. Most of Britain's bird observatories are situated on promontories or small islands, often with accommodation in old lighthouse buildings. Sandwich Bay is - to borrow Monty Python's catch phrase - something completely different. I realized this when I had to stop at a kiosk and buy a ticket to enter The Estate, and then drove onwards - straight past the observatory, as it happens - and

Little tern

Sanderling

Waxwing

Straight into a golf course. Round the club house and out again, I pulled into a lay-by and considered the only other immediately visible habitat: cultivated farmland surrounded by a barbed wire fence. This wasn't getting any better! A wild place? I thought not.

The fact is, a first impression of Sandwich Bay may well be somewhat off putting (unless putting - and other golfy activities - is what you're into). Almost the whole area is indeed "private" and, at a glance, it looks pretty flat and unpromising. The reality though is much more intriguing, as I discovered during the rest of my day, once I had found the Observatory, got a little map, and followed advice on how to explore. The more I saw, the more I liked it. As it happens, I have always rather enjoyed incongruity in wildlife. Finding a rare flower on a building site, or a good bird on a sewage farm. Such experiences are the very essence of Sandwich Bay. You might have to dodge

found myself in a wide tree-lined avenue with houses so grand that they looked as if they belonged more in Hollywood than east Kent. As I continued down to the sea front, the movie image strengthened. I didn't know if these huge buildings were mansions or hotels, but one thing they had in common: they all seemed deserted and lifeless. Empty and yet not derelict. Exactly like an enormous back lot at a film studio. As I stopped the car and got out, I actually felt nervous. Was I allowed to park there? Could I look in that garden, or would I be trespassing? I decided not to risk it. I got back in my car and drove back the other way.

Broomrape *Orobanche caryophyllacea*

Sea holly with broomrape *Orobanche amethystea*

wayward tee shots to enjoy the orchids, or risk the wrath of a guard dog to get a better look at a Pallas's warbler or a waxwing, but it all adds to the uniqueness, and the fun.

The other thing I like about the Bay is that it's not easy. You really do need instructions on where to go and what to look out for. (Available from the Observatory or the Kent Trust). If you set out on the full circuit you'll soon appreciate that it covers a huge area and a surprisingly wide variety of habitats. Yes, there are the man-managed bits - the gardens and lawns, the golf courses, the farmland - but there are plenty of more natural features as

Marsh helleborine

well - sand dunes with lizard orchids, damp hollows home to the marsh helleborine, patches of buckthorn and bramble, willow thickets, ditches and fresh water marshes. And that's only around the estate. If you really want to experience "the wild", take the coastal path out to Shellness, across unspoilt salt marsh, ending up on a classic shingle ridge, carpeted with viper's bugloss, sea holly and the exquisite sand catch-fly, overlooking the mudflats of Pegwell Bay. It's a long walk but if things are happening it is immensely rewarding; and if they're not, you'll still get a sense of achievement at simply having done it. Did I say the Bay wasn't easy? Be honest, it can be positively hard work.

And yet, I suspect that it is precisely the "weird and difficult" image of Sandwich Bay that appeals to the "regulars". It is a place that requires time, patience, and specialist attention: all ingredients that are increasingly scarce amongst many pager-led modern birders. It is also a place that encourages - indeed almost demands - a much wider knowledge of wildlife. It is significant that the Bird Observatory Reports devote almost as many pages to flowers, moths and dragonflies as they do to birds.

Jazz fans talk of a "musician's musician", meaning a player with a subtle and probably less commercial style that is appreciated more by his

Sand catchfly

Lizard orchid

peers than by the general public. Arguably Sandwich Bay is a naturalist's nature reserve. A wild place? Only partially. Full of wildlife? Most definitely. Weird? Certainly. Wonderful? Go judge for yourself.

Bill Oddie
Ornithologist and broadcaster

Sladden Wood

ON 15 MARCH 1978, the Secretary of State for the Environment made a decision which, to those not familiar with woodland conservation, probably seemed perverse and self-contradictory. He confirmed a Tree Preservation Order on a wood in Kent which was at that moment known to be lying flat on the ground. As decisions go it was as much historical as historic, and a medieval woodman would have been amazed that anyone could consider a wood or tree to have been destroyed just because it had been cut down - how else did you harvest them? A great deal has happened to our woods in the last 500 years, and the knowledge of their workings and the forces that have moulded them has, like so

Stoat

Bracket fungus
Coriolus versicolor
on stump

much else, slipped away. In a climate of opinion that seems to be polarized between those who see trees as crops that will not grow unless they are planted and those who see them as monuments that should never be cut, the case of Sladden Wood marked the return of a glimmer of common sense about woodland evolution.

Sladden - or the Horizontal Wood, as it is known by those locals who have managed to keep their sense of humour - lies on the north side of the Alkham Valley, just inland from Dover. It covers rather less than seventeen acres (seven hectares), but is the richest of a string of ash and maple woods that wind along the steep slopes of this chalky valley. The character of the country here, and of the plants and creatures that live in it, is absolutely dependent on this mosaic, on the alternation of wood and down and scrub.

All the woods have been cut and cropped in the past, yet the valley has almost certainly been under some kind of tree cover since prehistoric times and carries many of the more sensitive woodland flowers. Sladden has herb paris, green hellebore and half a dozen species of orchid, including Kent's special glory - the statuesque and elegant lady orchid. It also has nightingales, a network of traditional footpaths and walks, and the affection of almost the entire local population.

In 1977, this ancient community of natural and human interest passed into the ownership of a decidedly modern farmer, whose zeal for improvement was well known from elsewhere in the county. He set to work on the valley immediately, with the intention of claiming as much as possible of it for arable crops. He cleared the shelter belts, ploughed up downland and grubbed out the first few patches of woodland. The NCC and many local amenity groups, fearful for the fate of this beautiful and fascinating stretch of country, arranged a number of discussions with the owner, none of which brought anything but gloom about its likely future. And, on 23 November, just seven days before a meeting which had been specifically arranged to discuss its fate, the bulldozers moved into Sladden Wood. Acting with quite commendable speed, Dover Council summoned up a Tree Preservation Order that same day and tried to serve it on the owner. The events of the next few hours had - in more than one sense - all the characteristics of a Whitehall farce. The owner (who had, incidentally, omitted to get a felling licence for the larger trees) refused to accept the Order because, he claimed, he had mislaid his glasses. When they had been retrieved he attempted to go over to the official serving the Order but, in his counsel's

Green hellebore

words, 'there were obstructions in between them, and by the time he had got round them the last trees had been felled'.

Sladden Wood that winter looked as if a tank war had been fought in it. In their haste to get the wood down before the Tree Preservation Order was served, the contractors had dispensed with the niceties of tidy felling, and had simply pushed many of the smaller trees over, or snapped them off some feet above ground level. Even some of the larger trees had been treated in this way, sawn half through, then bent over and broken. By any standards that day's work was an act of gross vandalism against what was, by long custom, a public amenity.

Green woodpecker

carrying out his threat to grub out the stumps. The ground - at present deeply rutted and smothered with rampant weeds and brambles - will take a while to recover from the assaults of the bulldozers. But the seeds accumulated in the soil over the years are still there and will start to shade out the weeds. As for the trees themselves, they will bear the marks of the extraordinary woodwreck of 23 November for the rest of their lives. Yet in doing so they may, ironically, become more fascinatingly textured than they were before. If no more is done to them than a touch of tidying and thinning, in one hundred years Sladden Wood will carry a distinctive collection of dwarf pollards, sprouting sheafs of contorted branches only a few feet above the ground (perhaps like the famous trees of Burnham Beeches and Epping Forest, which owe their particular shapes to centuries of lopping for firewood). It will have become as much an historical monument as a natural one, a reminder of nature's magnanimous ability not just to heal over the results of our activities, but subtly to incorporate them.

Essay written by Richard Mabey in "The Common Ground" on the destruction of Sladden wood, and reprinted here with his permission.

Richard Mabey
Author and broadcaster

Yet the following March, at the time of the inquiry into the owner's objections to the Tree Preservation Order, the splintered stumps had already started to send up new shoots. The inspector at the inquiry accepted the NCC's argument that a tree remains a tree unless it is uprooted or killed, that 'the wood will return to a woodland appearance even without recutting of the stumps', and that 'the reasonable degree of public benefit which must be established before a Tree Preservation Order can be confirmed can be future benefit'.

Sladden Wood, for the time being, escaped outright eradication, and a High Court injunction was served against the owner to prevent him

Post Script

20 years after the wholescale felling described above, Sladden Wood has recovered and is now a Kent Wildlife Trust reserve, purchased in 1987. True, the regenerating trees are of an even age, but the species mix is still present, and the plants described by Richard Mabey, including the lady orchid, still thrive. It stands as a fitting tribute to the resilience of nature.

Smallmans Wood

SMALLMANS is a traditional Low Weald wood planted primarily with coppice hornbeam for charcoal, coppice chestnut and ash for fencing and farm vehicles and standard oak for building. In the past an enlightened soul had also planted some wild cherries and service trees. Like all woodland of its kind, it is a riot of bluebells and anemones in the spring. My father was a keen naturalist and ornithologist, and throughout my childhood I had walked the wood with him and learned about and enjoyed the beauty and the wildlife.

I inherited the wood in 1964. A year later the Kent Wildlife Trust asked me if I would be prepared to lease Smallmans as a nature reserve. I accepted. My father and I acted as the first wardens. I received the princely sum of ten pounds per year in rent. Woods certainly do not make their owners a fortune.

In 1983 we drew up a woodland management plan. We were both keen the wood should be regularly coppiced. I like the wood to look tidy with no dead wood lying around, straight paths for easy access, and chemical control of brambles - the Trust likes dead wood to be retained to encourage the invertebrates, winding paths with bays cut at irregular intervals to benefit butterflies and dislikes the use of chemicals. Despite such differences of opinion we have always come to an amicable compromise. The reserve became a very popular place for local people to walk their dogs in the 1980's, and I became concerned that it was becoming a people reserve rather than a nature reserve. The butterflies were flourishing but other wildlife, particularly birdlife was suffering. We solved the problem almost over night by banning not people, but their dogs.

I had a long and happy relationship with Mike Enfield, an enthusiastic lepidopterist, from whom I learned a great deal and I have enjoyed working with John McAllister as well as the army of volunteers who cheerfully give up their spare time to work in Smallmans. I would unhesitatingly recommend an owner of a potential reserve to enter an agreement with the Kent Wildlife Trust.

Charles Dawes
Owner of Smallmans Wood

Bluebells and wood anemones

Velvet shank fungus
Flammulina velutipes

South Swale

Shingle with stonecrop

AS THE brightly coloured beach chalets straggle westwards from Seasalter and stop by the Old Sportsman pub, the South Swale reserve takes over the coastline and runs west, a narrow strip of foreshore, sea wall and marsh, for some four miles round into Faversham creek near Nagden. At low tide this narrow strip expands as the sea runs out to expose half a mile of mud running out in a spur towards Shellness and the estuary.

In the summer, this is a busy place. Families play on the beach, children scramble across the mud, sailing boats scoot up and down the Swale, and walkers stride along the Saxon Shore Way. But go instead along the lane to Nagden, through the apple orchards and strawberry fields, walk the mile across the marshes to Castle Coote, and the beach will be all yours.

The summer colours are brilliant. The sides of the sea wall are white with wild carrot and the concrete of the barrier has bugloss growing in cracks. The beach above high tide is scattered with yellow horned poppy, steel-grey sea holly and sea cabbage.

Behind the sea wall the reed beds are a nesting ground for reed warblers and sedge warblers. Marsh harriers drift across from their strongholds on Sheppey to hunt the dykes, and

Reedbeds

Brent geese in flight

meadow brown butterflies stumble along in the grass. On a sunny day, with the sea sparkling, and Sheppey shimmering in the distance, the Swale is a delight.

But in the winter this is an utterly different place. The sea, the mud, the Isle of Sheppey and the vast sky combine into a bleak grey emptiness and the North wind drives against the sea wall. The beach chalets are boarded up, the sailing boats stowed away, and the beaches are empty. All the colour is gone. Flocks of finches scavenge for seed along the beach and now and then snow buntings will join them. Brent geese in their hundreds fly in formation across the grey sky and settle to graze on the mud. The vast numbers of shells on the

Yellow horned poppies

beach indicate the richness of the tidal mud as a food source, and it forms a feeding ground for a great gathering of dunlin, knot, curlew, godwit and plovers.

On the sea wall on a bleak February day, with the grey mud stretching out to a grey sea under an empty colourless sky, there is a gaunt and desolate beauty about the Swale that the colours of summer will never match.

John Leigh-Pemberton
Chairman of KWT since 1998

Spong Wood

AN OLD coppiced wood, on a north-east facing slope of the North Downs, this wood is a delight at any time - utterly peaceful, rarely penetrated by noise of road traffic or aircraft. It is a Site of Nature Conservation Interest, about half way between Canterbury and Hythe, half a mile west of the old Roman Road of Stone Street.

Spong - "a long thin piece of land" - was added to about 200 years ago as evidenced by remains of an old ditch and bank field edge well within the present upper western boundary and is now some 30 ha. in area, adjoining a small coniferous wood at its northern end. The bottom of the wood and the arable field beyond, sloping up to another strip of wood (Edards Wood), form a shallow valley extending north towards Petham, and passing Yockletts Bank a mile away.

There are a number of standard oaks, ash, and sweet chestnut in what is ancient broad-leaved woodland, with a profuse undergrowth of neglected chestnut coppice and other species.

Ramsons

Fungus *Entoloma euchroa*

intended to restore a regular cutting cycle. A start has been made, with glade clearing and ride widening, to allow more light in and encourage the rich flora present, including hazel, hornbeam, honeysuckle, bramble, broom and willow herb, all food plants for the wildlife present.

The spring is wonderful here, with carpets of wood anemones, primroses, violets, bluebells and ramsons. Orchids are found - especially lady, greater butterfly and hundreds of twayblades. There are large drifts of toothwort and herb paris is common. The latter is found with five, six and occasionally even seven leaves.

There is still evidence of the Great Storm of October 1987, which devastated much of the woodland of Sussex and Kent, in the large fallen trees which remain as they fell - with huge plates of roots, chalk and soil standing upright over the holes which were left as they were levered out of the ground, as their trunks were pushed down by the hurricane force winds. The policy has been to leave them to weather and decay naturally, a wealth of food and shelter for many insects, fungi and birds. Only those boles posing danger to people using the wood were removed. Records of coppicing go back to 1792, but this ceased in the 1980s, the Trust acquiring the wood in 1988. It is

Dormouse

Herb Paris

Little owl

On a warm day in summer as well as the profusion of flowers, there are many butterflies including white admiral. As it gets dark, if one is very still and quiet, badger families can be observed.

The wide variety of shrub and tree species allows a healthy population of dormice to flourish, though you are unlikely to see them as they are nocturnal and arboreal in habit. They have been monitored on a regular basis over the last 8 years as part of the English Nature Endangered Species programme, carried out by trained and licensed volunteers and wardens.

A visit makes a lovely day out. Walk through the wood, across the valley from the eastern corner, on a bridle path, up to a lane, left on this for a few yards to another bridle path into Edards Wood and a long gentle downhill walk, around the conifer plantation and two pretty cottages, then left to Spong Farmhouse, and back up what is now a "green lane" to the wood; turn into it again up some steps and find yourself a place to eat your picnic in one of the sheltered glades. In spring and early summer you are quite likely to hear jays, woodpeckers, various tits including marsh, tree creepers and turtle doves and maybe see a family of sparrowhawks trying out their wings.

Graham Miles
Honorary Warden

Stockbury Hill

The deceiver fungus *Laccaria laccata*

Stitchwort and bluebells

THE A249 at Stockbury is effectively a motorway where the traffic hurtles along oblivious of anything except its desire to make full use of the racetrack created by the County's engineers. I know. I use it all the time. What I did not know is that within a few yards of the maelstrom lies a strip of woodland which is being looked after by the Kent Wildlife Trust.

Invited by the Trust to visit one of their reserves I chose Stockbury Hill because it is wholly in my constituency and MP's are almost as territorial as robins when it comes to their own "patches".

I drove to the car park of the Three Squirrels pub to meet Dave Hutton who then led me by the kind of diversions loved by police and traffic planners on to a typical Kentish lane; narrow, overhung with trees and bounded by brambles and the lace flowers of elder, cow parsley and all the other variants whose names I have always been too lazy to commit to memory.

We stepped into the wood noting just how untidy nature is if she is left largely to her own devices. Fungi sprout from fallen trees. Rotten stumps serve better than the Halifax to provide homes for birds and endless other creatures and, of course, that surprisingly straight line of young saplings turns out to have sprouted from where the branches of a fallen tree have buried themselves in the soft leaf mould.

The Trust do not leave the reserve entirely to nature. They try to ensure that the canopy does not grow so thick that the many orchids for which the reserve is famous cannot find enough light to thrive on. Dave Hutton knows this area so well that he can count almost every orchid. He pointed out to me not only the plants which were carrying their flowers so proudly in the dappled shade, but also those which this year will not flower because the shade is too dense.

Birds, trees, butterflies, orchids and plenty of signs of badgers. Not a bad haul for a morning's stroll.

I hope that the Kent Wildlife Trust will continue to flourish and go on creating small corners of our country where the mad bustle of motor dominated life can be forgotten for an hour or two. Thank you for reminding me of your importance to our county.

Andrew Rowe
MP for Faversham and Mid Kent

Westerham Mines

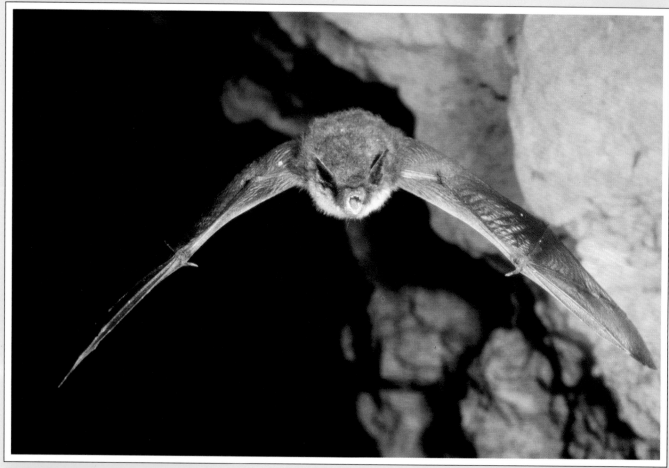

Whiskered bat

HOSEY COMMON lies to the south of Westerham. A north-south scarp contains entrances to a series of mines that were dug for building stone. No one knows exactly when they were dug, but the 17th century village church was built of stone from here as were many other buildings around the common and village centre. Perhaps the extraction was carried out by a small family business over many years. Three separate series of mines remain although there is evidence of further inaccessible workings to the south. The three existing series total about one mile of tunnel with pick and wedge marks to show that the passages were dug by hand and sledge marks to show how the rock was removed from the tunnels probably with the help of ponies. The tunnels are about 3 m wide and 2 m high. The good stone (Kent Ragstone) was in a narrow band at the bottom, but it is also possible that some usable stone or even sand for glass-making was taken from higher levels. This is a free-stone (it can be cut in any direction) and was probably worked underground, while still damp, since it becomes extremely hard when exposed to the outside atmosphere.

In 1972, Sevenoaks District Council decided that the mines were hazardous and should be sealed off. They were persuaded of the importance of the site, and handed over responsibility for it as a bat reserve to Kent Wildlife Trust in 1974. Since that time, the mines and the land surrounding them have been designated as an SSSI. Various experiments with vandal-proof bat grilles - financed by the WWF - were made and finally perfected in 1981.

Five bat species are regular in the mines: Daubenton's, Brandt's, whiskered, Natterer's and brown long-eared bats. It is odd that no other species has been recorded in the 40 years of survey. Although many ringed bats were refound in the mines, only one was found elsewhere, and that was a Natterer's bat eaten by a cat at Penshurst when it was at least seven years old. Primarily a winter roost, there is evidence of summer use. This includes odd bats resting during the night, but there may be increased activity in autumn, when large numbers of bats may collect in such sites during the night. The record winter count now stands at 59 bats counted on any one day but we know that there are many bats tucked away in crevices and that the population changes through the winter. Thus, the total number of bats relying on the site remains a mystery. It is likely to be many times the number actually counted on the Kent Bat Group's regular winter census visits, which are geared towards a standardised search method that will cause minimum disturbance.

Wrens nest just inside the entrances and foxes wander freely throughout the mines. The variety of invertebrate species is limited, but can occur in large numbers. Some fly species have proved of particular interest. Frogs and toads sometimes summer in the mine's cool and humid climate. Fungi grow in the mines on bits of wood or other plant debris, or on fox droppings. Growing in these unusual situations, they can prove a puzzle for the mycologist.

Tony Hutson
Senior Conservation Officer of the
Bat Conservation Trust

Westfield Wood

Stinking iris

WESTFIELD WOOD is a joy. It lies in that ever-narrowing strip of open countryside between Maidstone and the Medway towns. A small relic of an ancient woodland that would have once stretched seemingly to eternity. Step out of the wood and you step back into history. The Pilgrim's Way, with its origins in pre-history, runs along the edge of the Wood and the White Horse Stone, close to the southern entrance, once formed part of a prehistoric burial chamber.

What makes this wood so very special to me is its similarity to the Surrey downland woods of my childhood. In Westfield Wood I can freely relive those Sunday afternoon walks; rustling through the welly-high leaf litter under the beech trees that grow often so precariously on the scarp; building camps in the tangle of traveller's joy; hunting fearsome dragons that lived amongst the dark understoreys of yew. We were Pilgrims walking to Canterbury, collectors of Roman snails and junior eco-warriors - how dare they try and build the M25 across our toboggan run, we would stop them!

How Westfield Wood reminds me of those glorious, carefree, ever sunny days of childhood. The wood even has its own version of the M25 in the form of the High Speed Rail Link planned to skirt its edge - I will not let them fell one single tree!

There is a circular walk through the wood that allows me, just for a while, to forget life's little difficulties or at least put them in perspective. Here is a chance to soak up the wonders of the natural world; the music, the pastiche of colours, the complexities and inter-relationships.

The Reserve lies on a chalk spur between two coombes, features that owe their origin to the sculpturing processes of the last ice age. There is also a cap of clay-with-flints, a pot pourri of local materials, though principally clay and flint, deposited during the same period. Isolated Sarsen stones can be seen in odd places along the woodland edge, presumably cleared from the adjacent field. These stones, including the White Horse Stone, are cemented remnants of the once more widespread Lower Tertiary Sands.

At the southern end of the wood there is ash and beech high forest but with the ever-determined sycamore taking a hold. The scattered rootplates of fallen beeches lie as reminders of the October 1987 storm - monuments to the power of nature. In that brief moment nearly half of the standing timber in the wood fell. However, Westfield Wood has taken the 1987 storm in its stride, unyielding to this natural blip in its noble history. Today there is a tangle of regenerating trees and shrubs as the wood heals itself and a new process of succession begins. Ash is currently winning in the regeneration stakes. However, it is yew that is the climax vegetation here. Eventually the slow growing yew will outlive and replace the ash and beech leaving a woodland floor largely hostile to the survival of those broadleaf seedlings.

In this southern section grows the uncommon and extremely poisonous stinking hellebore - its smell inconceivably attractive to the early bees that hunt out its nectar. Not to be outdone in the perfume business you will also find the attractive stinking iris, known locally as dragon's tongue (so perhaps there really were dragons under the yew trees)! The use of the term stinking must be purely subjective as the smell of the latter is far less disagreeable. Another local speciality is the fly orchid, its velvety flower imitating so well a bluebottle fly.

Further into the wood yew is dominant but occasionally overtopped with an emergent canopy of ash and beech. Here the tiny goldcrest flits amongst the dense yew, hovering as it catches unwary insects. In the constant shade the ground flora is almost non-existent and scattered chalk fragments are a reminder of the thin nature of these soils.

The aptly named deadly nightshade has taken advantage of the disturbance and the gaps left by the 1987 storm. One is even currently thriving some 20 feet up in the branch of a dying beech. In the scattered clearings chalk grassland plants flourish, including salad burnet, hairy violet, marjoram, common milkwort and in summer, trillions of delicious wild strawberries. I wonder if just one tiny little strawberry going missing would upset the ecological balance?

Towards the top of the scarp the change to clay-with-flints is marked in spring by a display of

Fly orchid

bluebells. Early purple orchids grow here and the rare green hellebore. Coppiced ash trees include one that would make a sculptor green with envy.

Butcher's broom is a plant I find intriguing. Its name apparently originated from the use of the spiny stalks to scour butcher's blocks. It is an odd plant with no true leaves, instead it has leaf-like flattened stems that do the job of leaves.

One of my favourite shrubs has to be the spindle. Its hard, even-grained wood was once used to make spindles. The spectacular pinky-scarlet fruits hang from long stalks in summer and then burst open in the autumn to reveal the orange seeds inside.

Spindle berries

Yew berries

Dead wood is a speciality of this wood. Towering beeches, still magnificent in their dying years, provide high rise homes to a multitude of invertebrates and a desirable residence for a woodpecker family. There are ivy-covered logs for which a garden centre would pay handsomely and there is one log that is my very favourite. It lies halfway up the western edge and has a tablecloth of moss. It reminds me of the old green chenille cloth my grandmother always used to cover her best oak table.

As for the birds here, my inability to identify all but the most obvious bird calls is legendary but I have seen or heard woodpeckers, nuthatches, treecreepers, tits and watched a sparrowhawk overhead. As with classical music, I may not be able to identify the composer but that has never stopped me enjoying the composition.

I love this wood and I love to bring school children here. Most of all I love to bring youngsters from inner city London and especially those who are experiencing the countryside for the first time. They ask questions like 'who planted this wood' and 'where are the litter bins'. I hope they go away having experienced just a tiny bit of the magic of this wood and will forever remember the sunny, carefree day they spent at Westfield Wood - a wood without litter bins!.

Hilary Thomas
KWT Education consultant

Yockletts Bank

YOCKLETTS BANK is one of the best known, and for eleven months of the year, least used reserves in the Kent Trust portfolio. Each year hundreds of visitors make the journey to view the lady orchids. The telephone never stops ringing, the warden's wife never stops apologising for his absence and he arrives home to find terse notes: "Orchid man, Worcester - are the ladies out"?, signed "the home secretary". Orchid twitchers from every corner of the world call from every part of the country - the Irish tea planter just back from Sri Lanka; the New Zealanders 'doing the orchids of Europe'. Orchids engender a passion

Lady orchid

that dispels reason and demand from their wardens knowledge and flexibility that would test a saint.

"Is there a bus from Canterbury to Yockletts"?

"Are the ladies out? If I set off from Edinburgh after work on Wednesday, could you meet me at 6 on Thursday morning"?

"If I drive up from Launceston will I be able to do Park Gate, Yockletts, Queendown and Sandwich all in the day"?

Wardening Yockletts could almost seem a chore. However the job provides two great rewards. Firstly, the grandstand view of one of England's most spectacular orchids. Secondly, the almost solitary joy of delighting in the site for the other eleven months of the year. At risk of breaking this spell here is a Yockletts year that might encourage visits beyond the orchid season.

The year opens with tracks of fox and badger in the snow.

Spurge laurel flowers in February forecasting spring which comes in with violets, primroses, false oxlips and cowslips all hinting at the coming warmth. The bluebells push luxuriantly into the light. April sunshine adds brilliance to that particular yellow green that young beech leaves bring to southern woods. The canopy is alive with colour. A carpet of dogs mercury lies across the woodland floor and early purple orchids glare out of the deep green carpet and spring is here.

May is the month of the crinolined ladies, the sensuous purples of the fly orchids contrasting with the quiet mystery of herb paris.

Come June the lady orchid visitors have disappeared. At the top of the bank the common cow-wheat grows in profusion and yellow rattle adds another yellow to the miniature meadows. Insect life booms. Bright red cardinal beetles fly

Path with yellow archangel

Yockletts bank above a lane fringed with hedge parsley

across the paths. The larvae of these familiar beetles feed under the bark of trees for two or even three years before emerging. On warm days, the lucky visitor may see numbers of these glorious beetles.

The canopy has closed across the Droveway. Here in the shade the visitors escape the heat of the early summer sun and discover white helleborines and common gromwell growing alongside the paths. The greater butterfly orchids provide a thrill that compensates easily for the fading lady orchids. Nettle-leaved bellflower hints at the blue that it will add to the reserve's palette.

In the mid morning of July the heat doesn't hit until reaching the miniature meadow where butterflies dance to the buzz and chirrup of grasshoppers and bush crickets. As the sun sinks early behind Cox Hill Wood the solid hum of life gives way to furtiveness: rustling of leaves and scraping twigs reward the lateness of the hour with the presence of dormice and the sound of badgers foraging.

A hot August day, following rain, and the narrow paths seem quite tropical; bramble, bryony and briar reaching across to catch the face. The only other visitors are the Sunday strollers and picnickers.

During September the open areas are cut and raked, ensuring next year's harvest of wild flowers. Piles of grass cuttings form favoured basking places for the adders when the sun returns next year.

It's autumn and work begins in earnest. Each year a section of hazel understorey is cut by volunteers. The thicker pieces of wood are stacked in cord lengths ready for extraction as fuel while neater piles are made of bean sticks. The autumnal smell of wood smoke drifts through the reserve from the fire that burns the tops.

Lying along the eastern side of the valley Yockletts holds deep November frosts for days. The final flings of autumn colour are over during the month. Yockletts is a splendid destination. Walking towards the reserve from the Bavinge valley with the huntsman's horn blowing for home above Ittinge one is transported into another age. Yockletts Bank rising across the valley with the last rays of the sun catching the plume of smoke from yesterday's fire. The keen east wind carries ancient voices and the sharp music of hand bill on ash

Adder

Fox in winter

wood. The clip of horse shoes on the metalled road recalls a time within living memory when the local carter collected bobbins of pea and bean sticks from these woods and took them on to Canterbury market. A sylvan idyll when viewed from a distance.

Christmas holiday is a treat. Alone with the dog, spending a day without seeing another soul in a quiet valley which in five months time will become the Mecca of orchid spotting. Time is spent checking dormouse boxes, re-tying and repairing as necessary. The hard frost permits access for the trailer to take out coppiced wood.

Nick Onslow
Honorary Warden

•

The Making of the Landscape

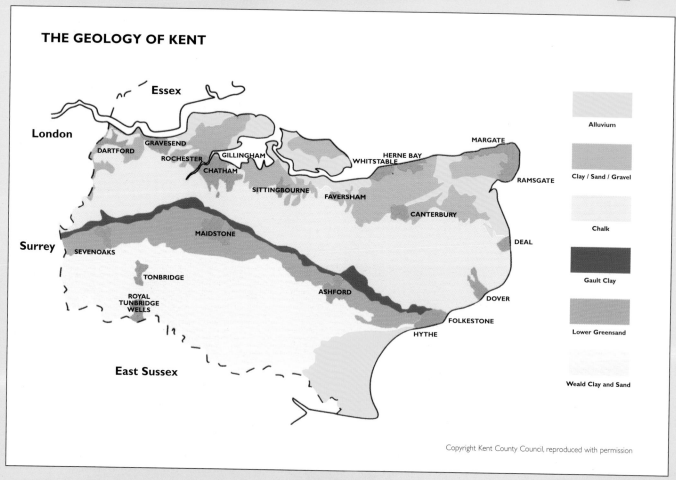

THE GEOLOGY OF KENT

Essex

London

MARGATE

GRAVESEND

DARTFORD

ROCHESTER
GILLINGHAM
HERNE BAY
WHITSTABLE

RAMSGATE

CHATHAM

SITTINGBOURNE
FAVERSHAM

CANTERBURY

MAIDSTONE

DEAL

Surrey

SEVENOAKS

TONBRIDGE

ASHFORD

DOVER

ROYAL
TUNBRIDGE
WELLS

FOLKESTONE

HYTHE

East Sussex

Alluvium

Clay / Sand / Gravel

Chalk

Gault Clay

Lower Greensand

Weald Clay and Sand

THE LANDSCAPE of Kent is as beautiful and varied as one can see anywhere in the world. If you leave Kent to cross the Channel and travel through France, or Belgium, or the Netherlands you can journey for hours with hardly a change in scenery. In countries like the United States you can travel for days through an unchanging landscape. It is true that you may then reach mountains with a grandeur and spectacle that Kent cannot match, but the county contains within its small area an amazing range of landscape, from lush woodlands and fertile marshes to a genuine desert, at Dungeness.

This variety stems from a providential conjunction in Kent of those forces which have moulded the land. All landscapes are a product of the underlying geology which shapes the framework of the land; the vegetation, which cloaks the bare rocks and the nature of which they largely determine; and the hand of man, which in Kent has greatly modified this vegetation cover and even the geology itself.

The geological foundations of the landscape

The story of the Kentish countryside thus begins with the laying down of huge thicknesses of sediment over immense periods of time to form the rocks of the Wealden series. The first Wealden

Kingsgate Bay

A typical dry valley on the chalk

deposits date from the beginning of the Cretaceous period some 135 million years ago. At that time the area which is now Kent was a great freshwater lake in which the fine sands and clays of the Hastings Beds accumulated. Conditions later became more sheltered and brackish and the sediments changed to form the clays and the limestones of the Weald Clay.

Further changes in the configuration of the land and sea then resulted in estuarine conditions under which the sands and clays of the Lower Greensand and Gault were formed. Eventually our area became covered by a clear, shallow sea. In it

there was a rich assemblage of planktonic animals and plants whose shells and other remains fell steadily to the bottom over a period of some 30 million years. Consolidated into a pure limestone, these remains built up a thickness of chalk which still approaches 1,000 feet today, even after erosion.

We know all this because some of the plants and animals which lived in these waters became trapped in the sediments and are preserved as fossils. We know the habitat preferences of similar species today and can thus infer the conditions under which their congeners lived in the past. The Gault Clay is particularly rich in fossils. The sea

Shingle at Dungeness

Erosion began to wear down the Wealden dome, but subsequent earth movements once more led to incursions and retreats of the sea and the laying down of the sands and clays of the Tertiary rocks. This started about 65 million years ago and continued intermittently until the beginning of the Ice Age some 1.5 million years ago. Most of the Tertiary rocks were laid down in the first 25 million years finishing with the London Clay. Thereafter erosion exceeded deposition and just some thin sands - the Lenham beds - were deposited at the end of the Tertiary, before the onset of the Ice Age.

The moulding of the present land forms

Unlike all of Britain north of the Thames, Kent was not covered by the great ice-sheets of any of the four major glaciations. The shape of the land before the Ice-Age was thus not very different from that we see now. Aeons of erosion had completely worn away the top of the Wealden Dome to expose all the succeeding layers of Wealden rocks right down to the Hastings beds. They formed the elevated core of the High Weald around which the exposures of the later rocks were arranged in concentric bands, like liquorice allsort. The soft Weald and Gault clays had naturally worn down faster than the harder sandstones of the High Weald and Greensand and the Chalk forming vales between the parallel ridges of the harder rocks.

Surprisingly all the major Wealden rivers, including the Darent, Medway and Stour, flow only partially along these vales, all cutting across the grain of the country and perversely breaching the Greensand and Chalk ridges to reach the sea. The

urchin, bivalve molluscs, shrimps and especially the little cuttle fish whose shells we know as belemnites, or bullet fossils, and the nautilus we call ammonites, which lived in this muddy estuary can all be readily found in the cliffs at Copt Point Folkestone and other exposures of the Gault in claypits inland.

Dinosaurs wallowed in the shallows and swamps of the Wealden waters. One of the very first dinosaurs to be described - Iguanodon - was first found nearby in the Wealden rocks of Sussex. Iguanodon, like most other dinosaurs, did not long survive for the Cretaceous period drew to a close with the onset of a prolonged interval of planetary disturbance as disruptive as any in the history of the world. The earth was racked by immense forces which lifted up the Alps and Himalayas. The Wealden deposits were also uplifted into an area of land forming an elongated dome.

East Stour, for example, rises little over a mile or so from the sea behind Hythe, yet flows nearly 50 miles in the opposite direction to reach the sea at Sandwich. This tortuous drainage pattern is thought to reflect its origin in radial steams flowing off the Wealden dome. Only subsequently, when erosion had created the clay vales, were the headwaters of the rivers able to flow along them as they still do today.

Although the great ice-sheets did not directly affect Kent, some honing of the land surface took place at this time. The climate then was sub-arctic and the ground probably permanently frozen and impermeable. The erosive effects of streams during thaws were thus much greater, carving out what are now usually dry valley and coombes in the Downs, and depositing much of the eroded material as deep spreads of gravel in the main river valleys. Thus were formed the Devil's Kneading Trough at Wye and all the little hidden, unexpected valleys on the deep slope of the Downs which add so much to the charm and richness of this landscape.

Coastal changes

During the glaciations huge volumes of water were locked up in the ice caps and sea levels were consequently much lower than at present. When the ice finally melted sea levels rose, so did the land as the great weight of ice was lifted off it, but eventually Kent was cut off from France as the Channel was flooded. At this time Romney Marsh was a shallow bay of the sea with the escarpment running from Hythe to Winchelsea as its shore. Ships could sail to Lympne until at least Roman times, when this was one of their main ports of the Kent coast, guarded by Stutfall Castle, now several miles from the sea. The Wantsum marshes were also sea at this time and Thanet an island; the important seaway guarded by the forts of Reculver and Richborough at either end.

Gradually sand and shingle spits built out from Winchelsea and Sandwich with salt-marshes forming behind them, just as can be seen in miniature today at Castle Coot in the Trust's South Swale reserve. Silting from the Rother and Stour, together with drainage starting in Roman times, gradually converted both estuaries to dry land. But not without many reverses. The Rother entered the sea at New Romney until a great storm in 1284 changed its course so that its estuary is now in Sussex, at Rye.

Thanet was again briefly an island after the East Coast floods of 1953. Similar sedimentation has added to the land of Kent in the estuaries of the Medway and Swale. Elsewhere land has been lost by coastal erosion. This has been particularly rapid in the soft London Clay cliffs of Sheppey and Herne Bay where the coastline has retreated hundreds of yards in historical times. Gardens can still be seen perilously overhanging the sea near Leysdown, clear evidence that the geological processes are still very active.

Vegetation cloaks the land

In the interglacial periods between the four major advances of the ice the climate was at least as warm as in this present interglacial, which we optimistically call the post glacial period. Plants and animals recolonised from their glacial refuges in Southern Europe and the flora and fauna of both Britain and Kent was far richer than it is now. In the last interglacial hippopotamus wallowed in the Thames and elephant, rhinoceros and lions stalked its shores. Large animals such as cave bears, bison, reindeer and giant elk probably survived the last

Reedbed at Stodmarsh

glaciation in places like Kent around the ice-fronts where tundra conditions prevailed.

When the ice retreated some 14,000 years ago and the climate began to grow warmer trees began to invade the tundras from the south. Birch, juniper and Scots pine first formed an open scrub forest, probably not very much different in appearance from Hothfield Common today. Wild horses and wild cattle grazed these grasslands and forest. As more warmth loving trees and shrubs such as hazel, oak, elm, ash and lime reached us from the south, so the forests grew thick and luxuriant. At this time all of Kent, hill and vale, even some of the coastal marshes, were covered in this continuous, impenetrable forest. Bears, wolves and wild boar were common in this forest as well as all our woodland animals which still occur today.

About 7,000-8,000 years ago the climate became much wetter, perhaps at least partially as a result of Britain becoming an island when the rising sea level finally flooded the land bridge to the Continent across the Dogger Bank. The recolonisation of plants and animals now became much more difficult and many which had got back in previous inter-glacials this time failed to do so.

Many of them, such as Norway spruce, rhododendron or little owl are thus unjustifiably reviled as "exotic aliens" when introduced by man, yet they are an integral part of our Western European ecosystems. One has only to look at any European field guide to see how many species range right up to the other side of the channel but have apparently never been able, unaided, to make the jump across it and colonise Kent.

The arrival of man

There were certainly human settlements in Kent during the Ice Ages and waves of colonists have come ever since. The oldest known human remains in Europe are the skull bones found at Swanscombe. This young woman was living on the gravel terrace of the Thames in the penultimate inter-glacial period. We do not know whether other Palaeolithic people survived the cold phases, but they certainly came back when the ice retreated to hunt the animals of the open tundras and park forests.

These Paleolithic peoples and the Mesolithic cultures which superseded them probably had relatively little direct effect on the environment. The thick forests and their fierce animals meant the Mesolithic peoples were probably forced to live mostly at the margins of lakes and at the seashore where there was also a ready source of food. They may have begun to clear some of the dryer woodland on the sandstone ridges using fire to drive or attract game and there is evidence that some heathlands date back to this time. The first major human impact came with new colonists, who brought agriculture to these island some 5,000 years ago.

These Neolithic peoples began a systematic assault on the forest which still continues today. They cleared the land for both pasture and cropping. The forest was almost certainly thinner and more easily felled and burned on the chalk and sandstone ridges than in the swampy vales so early clearances and settlements were in these places especially near the river gaps through the chalk.

Remains of their burial chambers, or long barrows, lined with stone megaliths, occur at Juliberrie's Grave near Chilham, Kits Coty near Aylesford and at Trottiscliffe and Addington. Their fields can still often be seen on downland, marked clearly by the shadows of their boundary banks, or lynchets, when the sun is low. There are good examples on Bilting Down in the Stour Valley. Aerial photographs have shown that such features are much commoner than previously believed and forest clearance was thus quite widespread at this time.

The Celtic Influence

Later colonists entering Britain around 2,500 years ago brought with them the knowledge of how to work iron. These Celtic peoples built the Iron Age hill forts at High Rocks near Tunbridge Wells, at Oldbury and at Bigberry near Canterbury where they resisted Caesar's Army in the century before Christ. Their new technology enabled them to tackle more difficult soils with iron ploughs and settlement expanded. But the thick forests of the clay vales remained almost untouched. Iron Age routes skirted the clay vales, hugging the foot of the Downs like the trackway,

Above Shakespeare cliff at Dover

much later called Pilgrims Way, which led from their settlement at Canterbury to the heartland of Iron Age England on the chalk uplands of Hampshire and Wiltshire.

Celtic Britain during its later occupation by the Romans seems to have made relatively little further encroachment on the great forests and wetlands which still remained. There was some drainage of Romney Marsh and Roman roads penetrated some of the forests, but mostly they stuck to the ridgeway routes like Stone Street and Watling Street.

The Anglo-Saxon Invasions

The clearance of the Wealden forest did not really get under way until the Anglo-Saxon invasions which intensified as the Roman Empire slid into decline. Their settlements were mainly sited in the already cleared lands and along the spring lines of the Chalk and Greensand ridges. It was these peoples who imposed the dominant pattern of land use which has persisted, with minor modifications, ever since in Kent.

Each village was largely self-sufficient with arable land on the better-drained soils, often on the ridges; meadows along the water course to provide winter hay for the stock, and unenclosed rough grazing - "waste" or "common" - to summer the stock. The parishes were, and still are, often irregularly shaped or even with detached parts to incorporate all three of these vital elements of the rural economy.

Cattle, sheep and pigs were often driven large distances to fattening pastures. Pigs in particular were driven every autumn off the open ridges and upland settlements into the deep Wealden forests to fatten on the rich harvest of acorns and beechmast. By this process cleared glades or "dens" in the Wealden forest were gradually opened up, each specific to its own parish back on the uplands whose flocks and herds used the same area every year. Thus Tenterden was the den of Thanet.

Gradually these clearances became permanent settlements and the Weald colonised. But it has never been cleared as completely as the rest of the countryside and still remains the most wooded part of England.

In much of Kent that land seems from the beginning of clearance to have been held or tenanted in small farms, rather than in strips in

Grazing stock created Kent's downland landscape

communally managed open fields as was common elsewhere. Other than in East Kent and in one or two other places where there were open fields, the Kent landscape was hardly affected by the enclosure movement of the seventeenth and eighteenth centuries. The pattern of the Kentish landscape was thus established by the end of the Dark Ages.

Development of Parklands

After the Conquest the land came largely into the ownership of King William's followers and the Church. Large areas were set aside for hunting as deer parks, commonly surrounded by fences, walls or ditches cambered on the inside so that deer could jump in but not out again over the steep outside bank. One can be seen at Godmersham. Knole Park, Sevenoaks, enclosed in 1456 still has deer in it. A survey of 1571 listed 54 deer parks in Kent. Some were formed with haughty disregard for the population living there. Eastwell Park, near Ashford, enclosed in Elizabeth's reign, diverted the main Ashford to Faversham road lengthily around its boundary eliminating the original village of Challock in the process. The village church still remains in the middle of the park, isolated from the new village which grew up to the north outside the park walls.

Later these parks came to be more important as pleasuring grounds and gardens around the great houses and many were specifically landscaped for this purpose in the eighteenth century. Capability Brown, the best known architect of such landscape designs, was responsible for Chilham Park and his protégé, Humphrey Repton, for several others in Kent.

The Creation of Wetlands

A key element in such landscaping was nearly always the damming of streams to make a lake. The numerous lakes then created are very important wildlife habitats for, never having been glaciated, natural open waters are very scarce in Kent. It is only in the present century that gravel extraction in the river valleys and subsidence due to coalmining, as at Stodmarsh, once more created extensive wetland habitats in the county. Previously there may have been extensive shallow swamps in the river valleys and coastland marshes but they have been subject to drainage since Roman times for the benefit of their fertile soils. The Open Pits lagoons in the shingle at Dungeness may be the only truly natural open waters left in the county.

Historical land uses

The great parks were enclosed to keep the deer in. Elsewhere the countryside was very different from today since most places were roamed by domestic stock which grazed everywhere that was not enclosed, including woodlands. Extensive tracts of land were by this means kept as open scrub woodland, heathland or downland. Many were used as rabbit warrens.

Woods which were managed for underwood from coppice had to be fenced to keep out stock and prevent the grazing of the regrowth, as did arable. In woods open to stock and in deer parks, trees were coppiced at a height such that stock could not reach the regrowth. The pollards produced in this way are still a feature of these parks and important habitats for many plants and animals especially lichens. Coppiced and pollarded woodlands were very important as they provided firewood, charcoal, fencing and a whole range of commodities vital to the rural economy. Wood was the main building material for ships and houses. Most buildings in Kent were timber framed with hazel wattle and daub or timber lap walls. Charcoal from coppice for iron smelting made the Weald the main industrial area of England until coke was discovered and industry moved into the coalfields.

This extensively used landscape of woods, deer parks, heath, down, marsh and arable persisted with remarkably little change from Medieval times to well into the present century. But in the last fifty years there has probably been more change in the Kentish countryside than in the previous five hundred. Most of this is attributable to a new agricultural revolution which had its beginnings in the last war, and it is this sudden and dramatic change that has given birth to the wildlife conservation movement.

Dr Bryn Green
Professor of Countryside Management at Wye College

(First published in Kent Wildlife Focus 1987/2 and 1987/3)

Mycena galopus

PHOTOGRAPHS

All photographs are by **John and Irene Palmer** except where stated below

Photographer	Page
John Buckingham	16(l & r), 18, 19, 20(l & r), 21(l & r), 27(l), 32(l & r), 33(l), 36(l), 37(l), 40(tl & tr), 72(r), 73, 79(l), 99(r), 101, 113(r), 115(bl), 119(r), 125, 126(l & r), 133, 143(r).
Julia Bracewell	8 (inset).
Ted Coleman	42, 43, 44(l & r), 45(l & r), 103(r), 131(r), 155(l).
Roy Coles	17.
Stephen Davis	23(t), 37(r), 57, 59(r), 67(l), 93, 94, 95(l & r), 105(l & r), 119(l), 140, 142(r).
Frank Greenaway	146.
Kent Wildlife Trust	66(r).
Nigel Matthews	8.
Andrew Ruck	107(l).

*Mycena galopus with
pinmould fungus on cap*